Oracle Database
Interview Questions and Answers

X.Y. Wang

Contents

3

Chapter 1

Introduction

Oracle Database is one of the most widely used relational database management systems (RDBMS) in the world, providing organizations with the ability to store, organize, and access data with high performance, scalability, and security. As the demand for skilled database administrators and developers continues to grow, it is essential to be well-versed in the intricacies of Oracle Database to excel in the industry.

"Oracle Database: Interview Questions and Answers" is a comprehensive guide designed to help professionals at various levels of expertise to prepare for Oracle Database-related interviews. This book aims to equip readers with the knowledge and confidence required to tackle challenging interview questions that cover a broad range of topics, from basic concepts to advanced features and best practices.

The book is organized into five sections: Basic, Intermediate, Advanced, Expert, and Guru. Each section covers a range of topics that cater to different levels of expertise, ensuring that readers can focus on the areas that are most relevant to their skillset and career goals.

The Basic section covers fundamental concepts and components of Oracle Database, such as SQL, data types, storage structures, and indexes. The Intermediate section delves into more complex topics, including PL/SQL, table partitioning, performance tuning, and backup and recovery strategies. The Advanced section discusses high-level topics like database tuning, Real Application Clusters (RAC), and Oracle Data Guard, while the Expert section explores even more specialized subjects, such as Oracle In-Memory Database Cache, SQL Plan Management, and GoldenGate technology. Finally, the Guru section addresses the most advanced topics, including high-performance architecture, Hybrid Columnar Compression, and advanced security measures.

Throughout the book, each topic is presented in a question-and-answer format, allowing readers to quickly locate and absorb the information they need. The questions in this book have been carefully selected and crafted to not only cover the theoretical aspects but also to demonstrate real-world scenarios and challenges that professionals might encounter in their work.

Whether you are a recent graduate looking to start your career in Oracle Database administration or development, an experienced professional looking to advance your skills, or an expert seeking to stay ahead of the curve, "Oracle Database: Interview Questions and Answers" is the perfect resource to help you achieve your goals. Let this book be your guide as you embark on the journey to master Oracle Database and excel in the world of database administration and development.

Chapter 2

Basic

2.1 What is the Oracle database, and why is it commonly used in organizations?

Oracle database is a relational database management system developed by Oracle Corporation. It is one of the most popular and widely used database systems in the world. The Oracle database is a collection of data stored in a structured manner, which can be easily accessed, managed, and updated. It provides a secure, scalable, and reliable platform for managing and storing data.

There are several reasons why Oracle database is commonly used in organizations:

1. Scalability: Oracle database is designed to handle large amounts of data and can scale to meet the increasing demands of an organization. It can support thousands of users and millions of transactions per second.

2. Security: Oracle database provides robust security features that help organizations keep their data safe from unauthorized access. It uses advanced encryption techniques to protect data at rest and in

transit. It also provides features such as access controls, authentication, and auditing.

3. High availability: Oracle database is designed for high availability, which means that it is always available for use. It can recover quickly from hardware or software failures, ensuring that data is always accessible when needed.

4. Performance: Oracle database is optimized for performance, which means that it can process large volumes of data quickly and efficiently. It uses advanced algorithms and caching techniques to speed up data retrieval and processing.

5. Compatibility: Oracle database is compatible with a wide range of operating systems, platforms, and hardware. This makes it easy to integrate with other applications and systems within an organization.

In summary, Oracle database is a powerful and reliable relational database management system that is widely used in organizations for its scalability, security, high availability, performance, and compatibility with other systems.

2.2   What are the key components of an Oracle database architecture?

Oracle Database architecture is based on the Client-Server Model, and it is divided into two main components:

1. **Oracle Database Instance**: The instance is the set of memory structures and background processes that function together to provide the functionality and services of the Oracle Database. An instance is created when a database is started, and it remains in memory until the database is shut down.

2. **Oracle Database**: The database is a collection of physical files that stores the data, metadata, and control information for the instance. It consists of one or more datafiles, redo log files, control files, and archive log files.

Below are the key components of an Oracle Database architecture:

1. **Oracle Database files**:

- **Datafiles**: Oracle stores the actual data in datafiles. These files are associated with a tablespace, and they contain the data for all of the database's tables and indexes that belong to that tablespace.

- **Redo Log Files**: The redo log files hold a record of all changes made to the database. This information is used to recover the database in the event of a failure.

- **Control files**: The control files contain metadata, such as information about the physical structure of the database and the names and locations of datafiles and redo log files.

- **Archive Log Files**: Archive log files are copies of online redo log files that have been filled up and archived. These files are used to recover the database in the event of a media failure.

2. **Oracle Instance Memory Structures**: The Oracle instance uses memory to store data and metadata that is required for efficient operation. The main memory structures are:

- **System Global Area (SGA)**: The SGA is a shared memory area that contains data and control information for the instance. The SGA is divided into several subareas such as the buffer cache, shared pool, large pool, and redo log buffer.

- **Program Global Area (PGA)**: The PGA is a memory region that contains data and control information for a single Oracle process. Each server process has its own PGA.

3. **Background Processes**: Oracle uses several background processes to perform various tasks. Some of the most important background processes are:

- **PMON**: The Process Monitor process is responsible for cleaning up failed processes and releasing resources that are no longer being used.

- **LGWR**: The Log Writer process is responsible for writing redo log entries to disk.

- **DBWR**: The Database Writer process is responsible for writing dirty buffers from the buffer cache to disk.

- **CKPT**: The Checkpoint process is responsible for signaling when a checkpoint has occurred in the database.

- **SMON**: The System Monitor process is responsible for performing instance recovery after a system failure.

4. **Database Connections**: A client connects to an Oracle database to use its services. To connect to a database, a client must provide a valid username and password, along with the database's connect string. The client can connect to a database using various interfaces such as SQL*Plus, Oracle Forms, Java Database Connectivity (JDBC), or Oracle Call Interface (OCI).

In summary, an Oracle Database architecture consists of an Oracle instance, database files, memory structures, background processes, and database connections. Understanding the architecture of an Oracle database is crucial for database administrators and developers to design, implement, and maintain an efficient database system.

2.3   Can you explain the difference between a logical schema and a physical schema in an Oracle database?

In an Oracle database, a schema is a collection of logically related database objects such as tables, indexes, views, etc. The schema can be further divided into logical schema and physical schema.

A logical schema is a conceptual view of the entire database or a subset of the database. It defines how data is organized and how the data is related to one another. It is represented by a data model, which describes the structure of the database and the relationships between the database objects. A logical schema is independent of any specific physical implementation.

On the other hand, a physical schema is a representation of the logical schema in terms of files and indexes on disk. It describes how the data is stored, accessed and managed on the physical storage devices such as hard disks, SSDs, etc. A physical schema is specific to a particular database system and its implementation.

To illustrate the difference between a logical schema and a physical schema, let's consider an example of a simple ecommerce database. The logical schema for such a database may include tables such as Customers, Orders, Products, and Suppliers. The relationships between these tables may be represented using a data model such as an

Entity-Relationship (ER) diagram.

The physical schema for the same ecommerce database may comprise of actual data files containing the data of the tables, indexes for these tables, and configuration parameters that specify how the database engine interacts with the storage devices. The storage devices themselves may include hard disks, SSDs, or other storage media.

In summary, the logical schema defines the concepts and relationships between the data, while the physical schema defines how the data is stored and accessed on disk. Understanding the difference between these two is essential for efficient and effective database design and administration.

2.4   What is SQL and how is it used in Oracle databases?

SQL (Structured Query Language) is a programming language used to communicate with and manipulate data stored in relational databases such as Oracle databases. Oracle databases are widely used in enterprise-level applications for their scalability, reliability, and security features.

SQL is used in Oracle databases for a variety of functions, including:

1. Retrieving data - SQL queries can retrieve specific data that meets certain criteria or conditions from a table or multiple tables.

Example:

```
SELECT * FROM employees WHERE department = 'Sales';
```

This query retrieves all the information from the employees table where the department is 'Sales'.

2. Inserting data - SQL is used to insert new data into a table.

Example:

```
INSERT INTO employees (name, department, salary) VALUES ('John_Smith', '
    Marketing', 50000);
```

This query inserts a new record into the employees table with the name 'John Smith', department 'Marketing', and salary 50000.

3. Updating data - SQL is used to update existing data in a table.

Example:

```
UPDATE employees SET salary = 55000 WHERE name = 'John␣Smith';
```

This query updates the salary of the employee named 'John Smith' to 55000.

4. Deleting data - SQL is used to delete records from a table.

Example:

```
DELETE FROM employees WHERE department = 'Marketing';
```

This query deletes all records from the employees table where the department is 'Marketing'.

In addition to these basic functions, SQL can also be used to create and modify database objects such as tables, views, and procedures.

Overall, SQL is a powerful tool for managing and manipulating large amounts of data in Oracle databases.

2.5 What are the main data types supported by Oracle databases?

Oracle databases support a wide variety of data types depending on the need and the data that needs to be stored. The common data types supported by Oracle databases are:

1. Numeric data types - These data types are used to store numbers. Oracle supports various numeric data types ranging from integers to floating-point numbers. The numeric data types in Oracle are:

- NUMBER(precision, scale): This data type is used to store a fixed-point number with precision and scale. The precision denotes the total number of digits that can be stored, and the scale denotes the number of decimal places.

- INTEGER: This data type is used to store whole numbers with signed values. The range of values for an INTEGER is from -2147483648 to 2147483647.

- FLOAT(precision): This data type is used to store a floating-point number with precision. The precision denotes the total number of digits that can be stored.

- BINARY_FLOAT: This data type is used to store single-precision floating-point numbers.

- BINARY_DOUBLE: This data type is used to store double-precision floating-point numbers.

2. Character data types - These data types are used to store text values. Oracle supports various character data types ranging from single characters to large text blocks. The character data types in Oracle are:

- CHAR(size): This data type is used to store fixed-length character strings. The size denotes the number of characters that can be stored.

- VARCHAR2(size): This data type is used to store variable-length character strings. The size denotes the maximum number of characters that can be stored.

- CLOB: This data type is used to store large character strings.

3. Date and time data types - These data types are used to store date and time values. Oracle supports various date and time data types. The date and time data types in Oracle are:

- DATE: This data type is used to store date and time values with a precision of up to a second.

- TIMESTAMP: This data type is used to store date and time values with a precision of up to a fractional second.

- INTERVAL: This data type is used to store duration values.

4. LOB data types - These data types are used to store large objects

such as images, audio, and video files. Oracle supports various LOB data types. The LOB data types in Oracle are:

- BLOB: This data type is used to store binary large objects.

- BFILE: This data type is used to store large binary files.

Overall, Oracle databases provide a wide range of data types to support different types of data and data processing needs.

2.6 Can you describe the basic structure of a SQL SELECT statement?

A SELECT statement is used to retrieve data from one or more tables in a database. It retrieves a set of records or rows that match a specified condition or set of conditions.

The basic structure of a SELECT statement is as follows:

```
SELECT [column(s)/expression(s)]
FROM [table(s)/view(s)]
WHERE [condition(s)]
GROUP BY [column(s)]
HAVING [condition(s)]
ORDER BY [column(s)] [ASC/DESC];
```

Let's break down each component of the statement:

- 'SELECT': This is the keyword used to specify the columns or expressions that you want to retrieve from the table. If you want to retrieve all columns, you can use a '*' instead of specifying individual column names.

- 'FROM': This is the keyword used to specify the table or view from which you want to retrieve the data. You can also specify multiple tables or views by separating them with commas.

- 'WHERE': This is the keyword used to specify the condition or set of conditions that must be met to retrieve the data. You can use comparison operators like '=', '!=', '<', '>', '<=', '>=', logical operators like 'AND', 'OR', and wildcard characters like '

- 'GROUP BY': This is the keyword used to group the results by one or more columns. This is typically used with aggregate functions like 'SUM', 'AVG', 'MIN', 'MAX', or 'COUNT' to summarize data.

- 'HAVING': This is the keyword used to filter the results based on aggregated column values. This is similar to the 'WHERE' clause but applies to groups of rows rather than individual rows.

- 'ORDER BY': This is the keyword used to sort the results by one or more columns. You can specify 'ASC' (ascending) or 'DESC' (descending) for each column to control the order of the results.

Here is an example of a simple SELECT statement that retrieves all columns from a table called 'employees':

```
SELECT *
FROM employees;
```

And here is an example of a more complex SELECT statement that retrieves only the 'department_id' and the sum of the 'salary' for each department with a sum of at least 1 million, grouped by 'department_id', and ordered by the sum of salaries in descending order:

```
SELECT department_id, SUM(salary)
FROM employees
GROUP BY department_id
HAVING SUM(salary) > 1000000
ORDER BY SUM(salary) DESC;
```

2.7 What is the purpose of the Data Dictionary in Oracle databases?

The Data Dictionary in Oracle databases is a collection of metadata that describes the structure and attributes of database objects. It serves as an authoritative source of information for the database system about the objects within it. Specifically, the Data Dictionary can be used to answer queries about the following:

1. Tables: Information about tables in the database such as their columns, constraints, and indexes. For example, you can use the Data Dictionary to find out which tables in the database have a specific column, or to check the data type of a column.

2. Views: Information about views in the database such as their defining SQL and the tables and columns they reference. For example, you can use the Data Dictionary to determine which views in the database reference a specific table.

3. Indexes: Information about indexes in the database such as their columns and type (e.g. B-tree or bitmap). For example, you can use the Data Dictionary to find out which columns are indexed in a particular table.

4. Constraints: Information about constraints in the database such as their type (e.g. primary key, foreign key, check), and the tables and columns they affect. For example, you can use the Data Dictionary to find out which columns are subject to foreign key constraints.

5. Users: Information about users in the database such as their privileges and roles. For example, you can use the Data Dictionary to find out which users have privileges to update a particular table.

6. Privileges: Information about privileges granted to users in the database. For example, you can use the Data Dictionary to find out which privileges are granted to a particular user.

Developers and DBAs use the Data Dictionary extensively during application development, database design, and administration tasks. For example, when creating a new table or view, the Data Dictionary can be used to ensure that the table or view definition conforms to naming conventions and requirements for security and access control. Similarly, the Data Dictionary can be used to check for existing indexes or constraints that might conflict with new database objects being created. Overall, the Data Dictionary is an essential tool for working with Oracle databases and managing their objects.

2.8   What are the primary storage structures in an Oracle database, and what are their functions?

Oracle Database uses several storage structures to store and manage data. The primary storage structures include:

1. Datafiles: A datafile is a physical file on disk that stores the actual data of an Oracle database. Each tablespace in an Oracle database consists of one or more datafiles. Datafiles are used to store database objects such as tables, indexes, and stored procedures.

2. Redo log files: A redo log file is a circular buffer that records all changes made to the database. The buffer is used to recover the database in case of a system failure. Redo log files are stored on disk and are used to ensure transactional consistency in the database.

3. Control files: A control file is a small binary file that is used to manage the metadata of the database. The control file contains information about the database name, location of datafiles, redo log files, and other important details about the database. There are usually multiple control files kept in different locations to help prevent data loss in case of a failure.

4. Tablespaces: A tablespace is a logical storage structure made up of one or more datafiles. Objects in the database like tables, indexes, stored procedures, etc., are stored in tablespaces. Tablespaces help manage the physical storage of objects.

5. Segments: A segment is a logical storage structure that represents a database object, such as a table, index, or stored procedure. Segments are composed of one or more extents.

6. Extents: An extent is a logical storage unit made up of a set of contiguous data blocks in a datafile. An extent corresponds to a set of data blocks that are allocated to a specific segment.

The primary functions of these storage structures are:

1. Storage and retrieval of data: Datafiles are used to store the actual data of an Oracle database. Segments and extents help manage the physical storage of database objects.

2. Maintaining database consistency: Redo log files are used to maintain transactional consistency in a database. Control files contain metadata about the database and help prevent data loss in case of a failure.

3. Performance optimization: Tablespaces and segments can be optimized to improve the performance of the database.

Examples of how these structures are used in an Oracle database:

1. Datafiles: Let's say, for example, that you have a table called "employees" that you want to add to an Oracle database. To do this, you would create a tablespace to store the table and then create a datafile within that tablespace to hold the data for the "employees" table.

2. Redo log files: When a user updates a record in the "employees" table, the change is recorded in the redo log files. If a system failure occurs, the redo log files can be used to recover the changes made to the database.

3. Control files: Control files contain metadata about the database, such as the database name, the location of the datafiles, and information about the redo log files. Control files help maintain database integrity and prevent data loss in case of a failure.

4. Tablespaces: Tablespaces can be created or altered to improve the performance of the database. For example, you might create a new tablespace that is stored on high-performance disk drives to improve the speed of data access.

5. Segments: If you have a table called "employees" that contains millions of records, you might create separate segments for each department to improve the performance of queries that relate to specific departments.

6. Extents: Extents are allocated to segments as needed. For example, if you add more data to the "employees" table, Oracle Database might allocate a new extent to the table to store the additional data.

2.9 What is the difference between a table and a view in an Oracle database?

In Oracle database, a table is a physical storage structure that contains rows and columns, where the data is stored permanently. On the other hand, a view is a virtual table that is derived from one or more tables or views in the database. A view does not store any data, rather it displays the data from one or more underlying tables or views as if they were a single table.

Let's look at some of the differences between a table and a view in Oracle database:

1. Data storage: A table is a physical storage structure where the data is stored permanently on the disk. Whereas, a view is a logical structure that does not store any data on the disk, instead, it retrieves the data from the underlying tables or views.

2. Definition: A table has a distinct name and unique set of columns with a fixed data type and size. The columns in a table can be modified using Data Manipulation Language (DML) statements like INSERT, UPDATE, and DELETE. Whereas, a view is defined by a query that retrieves data from one or more tables or views. The columns in a view are not fixed and can be changed by modifying the underlying query. However, DML statements cannot be used directly on a view, and any changes to the data require modifying the underlying tables or views.

3. Data Access: Tables are used to store and manipulate data, whereas views are used to simplify data retrieval by abstracting the complexity of the underlying tables or views. A view can be used to hide certain columns or rows from the user based on their permission levels or business requirements.

4. Performance: A view may improve the performance of a query if it contains complex joins or aggregations that require significant computation. By storing the results of the computation in a view, the data can be accessed faster than by performing the computation each time the query is run. However, creating too many views may degrade the performance of the database as it requires more system resources.

In conclusion, tables and views in Oracle database serve different purposes. Tables are used for storing, modifying and managing data while views are used for querying and manipulating data from one or more underlying tables or views. A table is a physical structure, and a view is a logical structure. Understanding the differences between the two and their respective use cases will help in designing efficient and scalable database systems.

2.10   How do indexes work in Oracle databases, and why are they important?

Indexes in Oracle databases work by providing a way to quickly lookup data based on the values of certain columns. They are important because they can significantly improve the performance of queries by reducing the amount of data that needs to be scanned or joined.

When a query is executed, Oracle's query optimizer determines the most efficient way to retrieve the necessary data. If the optimizer determines that an index can be used to retrieve the data more efficiently than scanning the entire table, it will use the index to do so.

Indexes are created on one or more columns in a table, and consist of a data structure that maps the values in those columns to the physical location of the corresponding rows in the table. When a query is executed that uses the indexed column(s), Oracle can use the index to locate the relevant rows without having to scan the entire table.

For example, consider a table called 'employee' with columns 'id', 'name', 'age', and 'salary'. If we frequently search for employees based on their 'name', we could create an index on the 'name' column:

```
CREATE INDEX idx_employee_name ON employee(name);
```

When a query is executed that includes a 'WHERE' clause filtering on the 'name' column, Oracle can use the index to locate the relevant rows more efficiently than scanning the entire 'employee' table.

Indexes are also important because they can be used to enforce constraints such as primary and unique keys. When a primary key is defined on a table, Oracle automatically creates an index on the relevant column(s) to ensure that the values are unique and can be quickly looked up.

Overall, indexes are a critical component of Oracle databases as they can significantly improve the performance of queries by reducing the amount of data that needs to be scanned or joined, and are often used to enforce constraints such as primary and unique keys.

2.11   What is a primary key, and why is it important in database design?

A primary key is a field or set of fields in a relational database table that uniquely identifies each record in the table. The primary key is used to enforce data integrity and ensure that each record can be uniquely identified and accessed.

Here are some key characteristics of primary keys:

Uniqueness: Each record in the table must have a unique primary key value. This ensures that no two records in the table can have the same primary key value.

Non-nullability: The primary key field cannot contain null values. This ensures that each record in the table has a valid primary key value.

Stability: The primary key value should not change over time. This ensures that the primary key can be used to uniquely identify a record even if its data changes.

Commonly, primary keys are created using an auto-incrementing integer column or a unique identifier, such as a GUID or UUID. Here is an example of a primary key definition in a SQL CREATE TABLE statement:

```
CREATE TABLE customers (
  customer_id INT PRIMARY KEY,
  customer_name VARCHAR(50),
  email VARCHAR(100),
  phone VARCHAR(20)
);
```

In this example, the customer_id column is defined as the primary key for the customers table.

Primary keys are important in database design because they provide a way to uniquely identify and access records in the table. By using a primary key, you can ensure that each record in the table is unique, and you can enforce data integrity constraints such as referential integrity. Primary keys also provide a way to join tables together and create relationships between them, which is important for data analysis and reporting. Overall, primary keys are a fundamental aspect of relational database design and play a critical role in ensuring data accuracy and consistency.

2.12   What is the purpose of a foreign key in a relational database?

A foreign key is a column or set of columns in one table that refers to the primary key of another table. The purpose of a foreign key is to enforce referential integrity between the two tables. This means that a value in the foreign key column(s) of one table must match a value in the primary key column(s) of another table, or the transaction will fail.

For example, consider a relational database with two tables: "Customers" and "Orders". The "Customers" table has a primary key of "CustomerID", and the "Orders" table has a foreign key of "CustomerID" that refers to the "CustomerID" column in the "Customers" table. This means that when inserting a new order into the "Orders" table, the value of the "CustomerID" column in the new order must exist in the "CustomerID" column of the "Customers" table, or the transaction will fail.

Foreign keys help maintain the integrity and consistency of data in a database. They prevent the insertion of invalid data by ensuring that each foreign key value has a corresponding primary key value in another table. In addition, foreign keys can be used to JOIN tables, allowing for more complex queries and data analysis.

Here's an example of how foreign keys are used in SQL code:

```
CREATE TABLE Customers (
    CustomerID int PRIMARY KEY,
    Name varchar(255)
);

CREATE TABLE Orders (
    OrderID int PRIMARY KEY,
    CustomerID int,
    OrderDate date,
    FOREIGN KEY (CustomerID) REFERENCES Customers(CustomerID)
);
```

In this example, the "Orders" table has a foreign key constraint on the

"CustomerID" column, which references the "CustomerID" column in the "Customers" table. This ensures that every order in the "Orders" table is associated with a valid customer in the "Customers" table.

2.13 Can you explain the different types of JOIN operations in SQL, and when to use them?

In SQL, JOIN operations are used to combine the data from two or more related tables into a single result set. There are several types of JOIN operations in SQL, each of which is appropriate for different situations. The common types of JOIN operations are:

1. INNER JOIN: also known as EQUI JOIN, returns all the matching rows between two tables based on a specified condition. It's the most commonly used type of JOIN. Here's an example of an INNER JOIN:

```
SELECT *
FROM Orders
INNER JOIN Customers
ON Orders.CustomerID = Customers.CustomerID;
```

This query returns all the orders that are associated with a particular customer.

2. LEFT JOIN: returns all the rows from the left table and matching rows from the right table based on a specified condition. If there are no matching rows in the right table, the result will contain NULL values. Here's an example of a LEFT JOIN:

```
SELECT *
FROM Customers
LEFT JOIN Orders
ON Customers.CustomerID = Orders.CustomerID;
```

This query returns all the customers, including those who have not placed any orders.

3. RIGHT JOIN: returns all the rows from the right table and matching rows from the left table based on a specified condition. If there are no matching rows in the left table, the result will contain NULL values. Here's an example of a RIGHT JOIN:

```
SELECT *
FROM Orders
RIGHT JOIN Customers
ON Orders.CustomerID = Customers.CustomerID;
```

This query returns all the orders, including those that have not been placed by any customers.

4. FULL OUTER JOIN: returns all the rows from both tables, including those that do not have matching rows in the other table. If there is no matching row in one of the tables, the result will contain NULL values. Here's an example of a FULL OUTER JOIN:

```
SELECT *
FROM Customers
FULL OUTER JOIN Orders
ON Customers.CustomerID = Orders.CustomerID;
```

This query returns all the customers and orders, including those that do not have any matching rows in the other table.

5. CROSS JOIN: returns the Cartesian product of both tables, which means all possible combinations of rows from both tables are returned. A CROSS JOIN does not require a condition as it returns all combinations. Here's an example of a CROSS JOIN:

```
SELECT *
FROM Customers
CROSS JOIN Orders;
```

This query returns all possible combinations of customers and orders.

In summary, the type of JOIN operation selected depends on the specific needs of the query. INNER JOINs provide the most common way to combine related data from two tables, while LEFT JOINs are used when certain data should be included even if it does not have a match in the other table. RIGHT JOINs are used similarly to LEFT JOINs, but with the roles of the tables reversed. FULL OUTER JOINs are used when all data from both tables should be included, even if it does not have a match in the other table. CROSS JOINs are less commonly used and specifically intended to return all possible combinations of rows from two tables.

2.14   What is normalization, and why is it important in database design?

Normalization is the process of organizing data in a database to minimize redundancy and dependency. It involves breaking down a table into smaller tables and defining relationships between them. The goal of normalization is to achieve data consistency and reduce data duplication.

Normalization is important in database design for several reasons:

1) Reducing data redundancy: Normalization eliminates the need to store the same data multiple times, which can save storage space and make data management more efficient. When data is duplicated, updating it in one place doesn't necessarily update it in all the other places where it is stored, resulting in data inconsistencies and potential data anomalies.

2) Improving data integrity: Normalization eliminates data inconsistencies and dependencies, helping ensure data integrity. By defining relationships between tables, it is easier to ensure that data is accurate and up-to-date.

3) Enhancing query efficiency: When a database is normalized, it is easier for the database management system to process queries efficiently. Queries require less computation, as the tables have been broken down into smaller tables with defined relationships. This can lead to faster query results.

There are several levels of normalization, including first normal form (1NF), second normal form (2NF), and third normal form (3NF). Each level has specific criteria that must be met in order for a table to be considered normalized.

For example, a table is considered to be in first normal form (1NF) if it meets the following criteria:

- Each column in the table contains atomic values i.e. it is not repeating any group of values and can't be splitted further - The values in each column are of the same data type.

To summarize, normalization is crucial in database design as it helps improve data integrity, reduce data redundancy and enhance query efficiency.

2.15   How do you create a simple table in Oracle SQL using the CREATE TABLE statement?

To create a simple table in Oracle SQL, we can use the CREATE TABLE statement. The basic syntax for the CREATE TABLE statement is as follows:

```
CREATE TABLE table_name (
    column1 datatype,
    column2 datatype,
    ...
);
```

Each column is defined with a data type and we can also specify any constraints on the column, such as NOT NULL, UNIQUE, or PRIMARY KEY. Here is an example of a simple table creation:

```
CREATE TABLE employees (
    employee_id NUMBER(5) PRIMARY KEY,
    first_name  VARCHAR2(50),
    last_name   VARCHAR2(50),
    email       VARCHAR2(100) UNIQUE,
    hire_date   DATE,
    job_title   VARCHAR2(50),
    salary      NUMBER(10,2)
);
```

In this example, we created a table called "employees" with six columns: employee_id, first_name, last_name, email, hire_date, job_title, and salary.

The employee_id column is defined with the NUMBER data type and is also defined as the primary key of the table. The first_name, last_name, and job_title columns are defined as VARCHAR2 data type with a maximum length of 50 characters. The email column is also defined as a VARCHAR2 data type but has the UNIQUE constraint, meaning that each value in this column must be unique. The hire_date column is defined with the DATE data type, while the salary column is defined as a NUMBER data type with a maximum of 10 digits, including 2 decimal places.

By executing this SQL statement, the employees table will be created in the Oracle database ready to store data. We can then insert rows of data into the table using the INSERT INTO statement, or we can modify it using the ALTER or DROP commands.

2.16   What are transactions in Oracle databases, and what are the ACID properties?

In an Oracle database, a transaction is a logically related series of database operations that are performed as if they were a single unit of work. Transactions are used to ensure data consistency and integrity, and to enable recovery in the event of system failures or errors. In a multi-user environment, transactions isolate concurrent access to data and enforce data locking and serialization.

The ACID properties are a set of characteristics that ensure database transactions are executed reliably. ACID stands for Atomicity, Consistency, Isolation, and Durability:

1. Atomicity: A transaction is atomic, meaning it is indivisible and all-or-nothing. Either all the operations in a transaction are completed successfully and the transaction is committed, or none of the operations are completed and the transaction is rolled back.

2. Consistency: A transaction ensures that the database moves from one consistent state to another. The data is transformed according to rules that ensure that it remains consistent, even if a transaction fails.

3. Isolation: Transactions execute in isolation from each other, which means that concurrent transactions cannot interfere with each other. They are isolated from each other using locking and serialization techniques.

4. Durability: Once a transaction has been committed, the changes made to the database are permanent and survive system crashes or power failures.

For example, suppose a user performs a transaction to transfer money from one bank account to another. The transaction would involve two database operations: debiting one account and crediting another account. If either operation fails, the whole transaction is rolled back, and both accounts remain unchanged. When the transaction is committed, the changes to both accounts are durable and can survive system failures. Moreover, the transaction keeps the data consistent and does not interfere with other transactions that may also modify the same accounts.

2.17   What is the purpose of the COM-MIT, ROLLBACK, and SAVEPOINT commands in Oracle databases?

In Oracle databases, the COMMIT, ROLLBACK, and SAVEPOINT commands are used in transaction management to ensure data consistency and integrity even in the presence of errors or exceptions.

- COMMIT: The COMMIT command is used to save all changes made to the database since the start of a transaction. Once a COMMIT command is executed, all the changes become permanent and cannot be rolled back. The COMMIT command is typically used when a transaction is completed successfully and the changes need to be made permanent, such as when a user submits a form in a web application.

Example:

```
BEGIN
  INSERT INTO employees (id, name, salary) VALUES (1, 'John', 5000);
  INSERT INTO employees (id, name, salary) VALUES (2, 'Jane', 6000);
  COMMIT;
END;
```

In this example, the transaction begins with the 'BEGIN' statement followed by two insert statements. The 'COMMIT' statement is used to make the changes made in the inserts permanent.

- ROLLBACK: The ROLLBACK command is used to undo all the changes made to the database since the start of a transaction. When a ROLLBACK command is executed, all the changes made in the transaction are lost, and the database is restored to its previous state. The

ROLLBACK command is typically used when a transaction encounters an error or fails to complete.

Example:

```
BEGIN
  INSERT INTO employees (id, name, salary) VALUES (1, 'John', 5000);
  INSERT INTO employees (id, name, salary) VALUES (2, 'Jane', 'invalid-salary'
       );
  COMMIT;
END;
```

In this example, the first insert statement is successful, but the second insert statement fails due to an invalid salary value. Since there was an error, the transaction is rolled back, and both changes are undone.

- SAVEPOINT: The SAVEPOINT command is used to divide a transaction into smaller parts that can be rolled back independently. When a SAVEPOINT command is executed, a specific point in the transaction is marked, and subsequent changes can be rolled back to that point without affecting the earlier changes made in the transaction.

Example:

```
BEGIN
  INSERT INTO employees (id, name, salary) VALUES (1, 'John', 5000);
  SAVEPOINT mysavepoint;
  INSERT INTO employees (id, name, salary) VALUES (2, 'Jane', 'invalid-salary'
       );
  ROLLBACK TO mysavepoint;
  INSERT INTO employees (id, name, salary) VALUES (3, 'Jack', 7000);
  COMMIT;
END;
```

In this example, the first insert statement is successful, and a SAVE-POINT named 'mysavepoint' is created. The second insert statement fails due to an invalid salary value, and a ROLLBACK command is issued to undo that change. The third insert statement is successful, and the transaction is committed, making both the first and third insert statements permanent.

Overall, the COMMIT, ROLLBACK, and SAVEPOINT commands provide a robust and flexible transaction management system that enables Oracle databases to handle complex operations while maintaining data consistency and integrity.

2.18   How do you grant and revoke user privileges in an Oracle database?

In Oracle database, user privileges can be granted and revoked using the 'GRANT' and 'REVOKE' statements respectively. These statements allow database administrators to control the permissions of individual database users and can be used to ensure that sensitive information remains protected.

To grant a privilege to a user, the 'GRANT' statement is used. Below is the basic syntax for granting a privilege to a user.

```
GRANT privilege_name TO user_name;
```

For example, to grant the 'SELECT' privilege on the 'customers' table to the user 'mike':

```
GRANT SELECT ON customers TO mike;
```

In the above example, the 'SELECT' privilege has been granted to the user 'mike' on the 'customers' table. The 'SELECT' privilege allows the user to read data from the table.

To revoke a privilege from a user, the 'REVOKE' statement is used. Below is the basic syntax for revoking a privilege from a user.

```
REVOKE privilege_name FROM user_name;
```

For example, to revoke the 'SELECT' privilege on the 'customers' table from the user 'mike':

```
REVOKE SELECT ON customers FROM mike;
```

In the above example, the 'SELECT' privilege has been revoked from the user 'mike' on the 'customers' table. The 'SELECT' privilege no longer allows the user to read data from the table.

It is also possible to grant and revoke privileges to and from individual database roles, which can be granted to multiple users. For example, to grant the 'SELECT' privilege on the 'customers' table to a database role 'readers':

```
GRANT SELECT ON customers TO readers;
```

And to grant the 'readers' role to the user 'jim':

```
GRANT readers TO jim;
```

In the above example, the 'SELECT' privilege has been granted to the 'readers' role and the 'readers' role has been granted to the user 'jim'. This allows the user 'jim' to have the 'SELECT' privilege on the 'customers' table.

Finally, it is worth noting that privileges can also be granted and revoked on system-level operations, such as creating and modifying database objects, and performing administrative tasks. These privileges are typically reserved for database administrators and are granted carefully, to ensure that sensitive information and operations remain protected.

2.19   What are the basic backup and recovery strategies in Oracle databases?

Oracle database provides various backup and recovery strategies that help in maintaining data availability, minimizing data loss due to failures or disasters, and restoring data in case of data loss or application errors. In this answer, we will discuss the basic backup and recovery strategies in Oracle databases.

Backup Strategies: 1. Full backup: A full backup is a complete copy of the entire database, including all data files, control files, and redo logs. It provides the most comprehensive form of backup but is also the most time-consuming and resource-intensive method.

2. Incremental backup: An incremental backup involves backing up only the data that has changed since the last full or incremental backup. It reduces the backup time and space required for backup storage.

3. Differential backup: A differential backup is similar to an incremental backup but only includes the data that has changed since the last full backup. It requires less time and space for storage than full backup but more than incremental backup.

4. Online backup: An online backup is performed while the database is still running and accessible to users. It uses the database's snapshot feature to take a point-in-time copy of the database. Online backup minimizes or eliminates downtime but can cause additional overhead on the system.

Recovery Strategies: 1. Complete recovery: A complete recovery involves restoring the entire database from a backup and applying all changes recorded in the redo logs since the backup was taken. It ensures that the database is restored to a consistent state.

2. Point-in-time recovery: Point-in-time recovery is a partial recovery that involves restoring the database to a specific time in the past. It involves restoring the database from a backup and applying selective redo log data to reach the desired point in time.

3. Media recovery: Media recovery is used to recover data files lost due to hardware or media failures. It involves restoring the lost data files from a backup and applying all changes recorded in the redo logs since the last backup.

4. Flashback recovery: Flashback recovery is similar to point-in-time recovery but uses Oracle's flashback feature to restore the database to a previous state without the need for a traditional backup. It works by querying and recovering data from undo segments that store a history of data changes made to the database.

In summary, Oracle databases offer a variety of backup and recovery strategies to protect against data loss, minimize downtime, and ensure consistent data availability. The choice of strategy depends on the specific recovery requirements, system resources, and backup and recovery time windows. It is recommended to implement a combination of backup and recovery strategies to ensure optimal data protection and restore capabilities.

2.20 What is the difference between DDL, DML, and DCL statements in SQL?

In SQL, DDL, DML, and DCL are three types of statements that are used for different purposes.

DDL (Data Definition Language) statements are used to define and modify the structure of database objects such as tables, views, indexes, and sequences. These statements include CREATE, ALTER, DROP, RENAME, and TRUNCATE. For example, the statement to create a table in SQL is a DDL statement:

```
CREATE TABLE my_table (
    column1 datatype1,
    column2 datatype2,
    ...
);
```

DML (Data Manipulation Language) statements are used to manipulate data in the database, such as inserting, updating, and deleting records. These statements include INSERT, UPDATE, and DELETE. For example, the statement to insert a record into the table created above is a DML statement:

```
INSERT INTO my_table (column1, column2, ...)
VALUES (value1, value2, ...);
```

DCL (Data Control Language) statements are used to control access to the database, such as granting or revoking privileges to users. These statements include GRANT and REVOKE. For example, the statement to grant a user access to a table is a DCL statement:

```
GRANT SELECT, INSERT, UPDATE, DELETE
ON my_table
TO my_user;
```

In summary, DDL statements are used to define and modify the structure of database objects, DML statements are used to manipulate data in the database, and DCL statements are used to control access to the database.

Chapter 3

Intermediate

3.1   What is the difference between CHAR and VARCHAR2 data types in Oracle databases?

CHAR and VARCHAR2 are both data types used to store character strings in Oracle databases, but they have some fundamental differences in terms of storage, performance, and functionality.

The main difference between CHAR and VARCHAR2 is the way they handle variable-length character strings. CHAR is a fixed-length data type, which means that it always allocates the same amount of storage for each string value. For example, if you define a CHAR(10) column, each value in that column will always take up exactly 10 bytes of storage, regardless of whether the actual string value is shorter or longer than 10 characters.

On the other hand, VARCHAR2 is a variable-length data type, which means that it allocates only as much storage as the actual string value requires. For example, if you define a VARCHAR2(10) column and insert a string value of 5 characters, it will only take up 5 bytes of storage. This makes VARCHAR2 a more efficient option when storing strings of varying lengths.

Another difference between CHAR and VARCHAR2 is their behavior when storing and retrieving data. Because CHAR is a fixed-length data type, it pads out shorter string values with spaces to fill the allocated storage space. For example, if you insert a string value of only 5 characters into a CHAR(10) column, it will be padded with 5 spaces to fill the remaining 5 bytes of storage.

This behavior can be useful in some cases, but it can also lead to unnecessary storage consumption and slower performance when dealing with large amounts of data. In contrast, VARCHAR2 does not pad out shorter values with spaces, which can improve performance and reduce storage requirements.

Here's a simple example to illustrate the difference between CHAR and VARCHAR2 in storing and retrieving data:

```
CREATE TABLE my_table (
    char_col  CHAR(10),
    varchar_col  VARCHAR2(10)
);
INSERT INTO my_table VALUES ('hello', 'hello');
```

If we query the table now, we will get the following results:

```
SELECT char_col, varchar_col FROM my_table;

CHAR_COL   VARCHAR_COL
---------- ----------
hello      hello
```

As we can see, the value stored in the CHAR column is padded with spaces to fill the allocated 10 bytes of storage, while the value stored in the VARCHAR2 column only takes up as much space as the actual string value requires.

In conclusion, the main differences between CHAR and VARCHAR2 in Oracle databases are related to their storage, performance, and functionality. While CHAR is a fixed-length data type that pads out shorter values with spaces, VARCHAR2 is a variable-length data type that allocates only as much storage as the actual value requires. Choosing the appropriate data type depends on the specific requirements of your application and data model.

3.2   What are the main differences between Oracle's DELETE, TRUNCATE, and DROP table operations?

In Oracle Database, there are three main SQL operations that can be used to remove data from a table: DELETE, TRUNCATE, and DROP. While they all have the same end result of removing data from a table, they differ in their implementation and effects.

1. DELETE: The DELETE operation is used to remove one or more rows from a table. It is a DML (Data Manipulation Language) statement. It can be used with a WHERE clause to specify which rows to delete. For example, the following SQL statement would delete all rows from the Customers table where the Country column equals 'USA':

```
DELETE FROM Customers
WHERE Country = 'USA';
```

One important thing to note about the DELETE operation is that it only removes data, it does not free up the space occupied by the data. The space remains allocated to the table, and will be used for new data inserted into the table.

2. TRUNCATE: The TRUNCATE operation is used to remove all rows from a table, effectively resetting the table. It is a DDL (Data Definition Language) statement. Unlike DELETE, it does not require a WHERE clause to specify which rows to delete. For example, the following SQL statement would truncate the Customers table, removing all data from it:

```
TRUNCATE TABLE Customers;
```

One important thing to note about the TRUNCATE operation is that it removes all data from the table, but it also resets any sequences that were associated with the table, effectively starting them over from their beginning values. Additionally, the space occupied by the data is freed up and returned to the tablespace, making it available for other tables to use.

3. DROP: The DROP operation is used to remove an entire table from

the database. It is a DDL statement. For example, the following SQL
statement would drop the Customers table, removing it completely
from the database:

```
DROP TABLE Customers;
```

One important thing to note about the DROP operation is that it
removes the entire table and all its data, as well as any associated
indexes, constraints, and triggers. This operation is not reversible,
and any data in the table will be lost permanently. It is important
to use caution when using the DROP operation.

In summary, the main differences between the DELETE, TRUN-
CATE, and DROP operations in Oracle Database are:

```
- DELETE removes individual rows from a table, while TRUNCATE removes all rows
    from a table.
- DELETE preserves the table's␣structure␣and␣any␣associated␣constraints␣and␣
    triggers,␣while␣TRUNCATE␣resets␣any␣sequences␣associated␣with␣the␣table␣
    and␣frees␣up␣the␣space␣occupied␣by␣the␣data.
-␣DROP␣removes␣the␣entire␣table␣and␣all␣its␣associated␣data,␣indexes,␣
    constraints,␣and␣triggers␣permanently.
```

3.3   Can you explain the differences be-
tween INNER JOIN, LEFT JOIN, and
RIGHT JOIN in SQL?

INNER JOIN:

INNER JOIN is a type of join that returns only matched records
from both tables. In other words, it only returns rows where there
is a match between the common columns of both tables. The syntax
for INNER JOIN is as follows:

```
SELECT column_name(s)
FROM table1
INNER JOIN table2
ON table1.column_name = table2.column_name;
```

For example, suppose we have two tables 'employees' and 'departments'. In this case, we may want to join the two tables to find the
department for each employee. We can use INNER JOIN to accomplish this as follows:

```
SELECT employees.name, departments.department
FROM employees
INNER JOIN departments
ON employees.department_id = departments.department_id;
```

The result of this query will be a table with two columns: 'name' and 'department'. This table will only include records where there is a match between 'department_id' in the 'employees' table and 'department_id' in the 'departments' table.

LEFT JOIN:

LEFT JOIN is a type of join that returns all records from the left table and only the matching records from the right table. In other words, it returns all records from the left table and only the records from the right table that have a match with the left table. The syntax for LEFT JOIN is as follows:

```
SELECT column_name(s)
FROM table1
LEFT JOIN table2
ON table1.column_name = table2.column_name;
```

For example, suppose we have two tables 'employees' and 'salaries'. In this case, we may want to join the two tables to find the salary for each employee. However, not all employees may have a salary record yet. We can use LEFT JOIN to accomplish this as follows:

```
SELECT employees.name, salaries.salary
FROM employees
LEFT JOIN salaries
ON employees.employee_id = salaries.employee_id;
```

The result of this query will be a table with two columns: 'name' and 'salary'. This table will include all records from the 'employees' table regardless of whether there is a matching record in the 'salaries' table. If there is a matching record, the 'salary' column will be populated. If there is no matching record, the 'salary' column will be 'NULL'.

RIGHT JOIN:

RIGHT JOIN is a type of join that returns all records from the right table and only the matching records from the left table. In other words, it returns all records from the right table and only the records from the left table that have a match with the right table. The syntax for RIGHT JOIN is as follows:

```
SELECT column_name(s)
FROM table1
RIGHT JOIN table2
ON table1.column_name = table2.column_name;
```

For example, suppose we have two tables 'salaries' and 'employees'. In this case, we may want to join the two tables to find the employee name for each salary record. However, not all salary records may have an associated employee. We can use RIGHT JOIN to accomplish this as follows:

```
SELECT employees.name, salaries.salary
FROM employees
RIGHT JOIN salaries
ON employees.employee_id = salaries.employee_id;
```

The result of this query will be a table with two columns: 'name' and 'salary'. This table will include all records from the 'salaries' table regardless of whether there is a matching record in the 'employees' table. If there is a matching record, the 'name' column will be populated. If there is no matching record, the 'name' column will be 'NULL'.

In summary, INNER JOIN returns only matched records, LEFT JOIN returns all records from the left table and matching records from the right table, and RIGHT JOIN returns all records from the right table and matching records from the left table.

3.4   What is the difference between an implicit cursor and an explicit cursor in Oracle databases?

In Oracle databases, a cursor is a database object that is used to manipulate and retrieve data from the result set of a statement. Cursors are classified into two types, implicit and explicit.

Implicit Cursor:

An implicit cursor is automatically created by Oracle when a SELECT, INSERT, UPDATE, or DELETE statement is executed. The implicit cursor is used to process each row that is returned by the query. The implicit cursor is managed by Oracle, and the programmer does not need to define or manage it explicitly.

For example, if a SELECT statement is executed in a PL/SQL block, a cursor is automatically created to retrieve the result set. The syntax for an implicit cursor is as follows:

```
SELECT column1, column2, ... columnN
FROM table_name;
```

Explicit Cursor:

An explicit cursor is a cursor that is defined and managed explicitly by the programmer. An explicit cursor is used when the programmer needs more control over the cursors, such as when the programmer needs to process multiple cursors in a loop or when the programmer needs to use cursors with DML statements.

The explicit cursor consists of four steps, as follows:

1. Declare the cursor

2. Open the cursor

3. Fetch data from the cursor

4. Close the cursor

The syntax for an explicit cursor is as follows:

```
DECLARE
   CURSOR cursor_name IS
      SELECT column1, column2, ... columnN
      FROM table_name;
   variable_name table_name.column_name%type;
BEGIN
   OPEN cursor_name;
   LOOP
      FETCH cursor_name INTO variable_name;
      EXIT WHEN cursor_name%NOTFOUND;

      -- business logic here

   END LOOP;
   CLOSE cursor_name;
END;
```

In summary, an implicit cursor is automatically created by Oracle when a SELECT, INSERT, UPDATE, or DELETE statement is executed, whereas an explicit cursor is explicitly defined and managed by the programmer. Implicit cursors are used for simple queries where

no additional control is required, whereas explicit cursors are used
when the programmer needs more control over the cursors.

3.5   What are the various types of con-straints in Oracle, and how do they ensure data integrity?

In Oracle database, constraints are used to define rules that ensure
the quality and correctness of the data stored in tables. The following
are the various types of constraints:

1. NOT NULL Constraint
The NOT NULL constraint ensures that a column cannot contain any
NULL value. It can be applied to any data type except for LONG
and LOB data types.

Example:

```
CREATE TABLE employees (
    emp_id NUMBER(10),
    emp_name VARCHAR2(50) NOT NULL,
    emp_email VARCHAR2(50) NOT NULL
);
```

2. UNIQUE Constraint The UNIQUE constraint ensures that each
value in a column is unique. A table can have more than one unique
constraint, and each constraint can be composed of more than one
column.

Example:

```
CREATE TABLE departments (
    dept_id NUMBER(3) UNIQUE,
    dept_name VARCHAR2(50) UNIQUE
);
```

3. PRIMARY KEY Constraint The PRIMARY KEY constraint ensures that each record in a table is uniquely identified by a particular
column or group of columns. It is a combination of a UNIQUE constraint and a NOT NULL constraint.

Example:

```
CREATE TABLE employees (
    emp_id NUMBER(10) PRIMARY KEY,
    emp_name VARCHAR2(50),
    emp_email VARCHAR2(50)
);
```

4. FOREIGN KEY Constraint The FOREIGN KEY constraint is used to establish a relationship between two tables. It ensures that the data in the referencing column or columns of a table matches the data in the referenced column or columns of another table.

Example:

```
CREATE TABLE employees (
    emp_id NUMBER(10) PRIMARY KEY,
    emp_name VARCHAR2(50),
    dept_id NUMBER(3),
    CONSTRAINT fk_dept FOREIGN KEY (dept_id)
        REFERENCES departments(dept_id)
);
```

5. CHECK Constraint The CHECK constraint is used to ensure that the data in a column meets a certain condition. The condition can be a logical expression or a subquery that returns a Boolean value.

Example:

```
CREATE TABLE employees (
    emp_id NUMBER(10) PRIMARY KEY,
    emp_name VARCHAR2(50),
    emp_age NUMBER(2) CHECK (emp_age >= 18 AND emp_age <= 65),
    emp_salary NUMBER(10,2) CHECK (emp_salary > 0)
);
```

These constraints ensure data integrity by preventing the insertion of invalid or inconsistent data into tables. They help maintain data accuracy, consistency, and reliability, and prevent data corruption or loss.

3.6 How do you create and manage indexes in an Oracle database?

Indexes play a significant role in improving the performance of database queries. When a query is executed, the database engine scans through the data to find the required results. With large amounts of data or when queries require multiple joins or filtering conditions, queries can become very resource intensive and take longer to complete. An index provides a structure for storing and retrieving data more efficiently, speeding up queries.

Creating an Index in Oracle Database

To create an index in Oracle Database, you can use the 'CREATE INDEX' statement. The basic syntax is as follows:

```
CREATE INDEX index_name
ON table_name (column1, column2, ...);
```

For example, let's say you have a table 'employees' with the following columns:

```
CREATE TABLE employees(
    emp_id NUMBER PRIMARY KEY,
    first_name VARCHAR2(100),
    last_name VARCHAR2(100),
    email VARCHAR2(100) UNIQUE,
    hire_date DATE
);
```

You can create an index on the 'last_name' column using the following command:

```
CREATE INDEX employees_last_name_ix
ON employees(last_name);
```

The above statement creates an index named 'employees_last_name_ix' on the 'last_name' column of the 'employees' table.

Managing Indexes in Oracle Database

Once the index is created, you can manage it using several commands.

1. Viewing Index Information: You can view information about an index using the 'DBA_INDEXES' or 'USER_INDEXES' views depending on the level of access you have.

```
SELECT index_name, table_name, column_name
FROM USER_IND_COLUMNS
WHERE table_name = 'employees';
```

2. Altering an Index: You can alter an index to change its structure or options using the 'ALTER INDEX' statement. For example, you

may need to add a new column to the index so it covers more columns needed for the query.

```
ALTER INDEX employees_last_name_ix
ADD emp_id;
```

3. Rebuilding an Index: In some cases, the index may become invalid or inefficient. In these cases, the index requires rebuilding using the 'ALTER INDEX...REBUILD' statement. For example, you may rebuild the index on a daily basis or whenever you add new rows to the table, especially when clustered.

```
ALTER INDEX employees_last_name_ix
REBUILD;
```

4. Dropping an Index: In case you no longer require an index, you can drop it from the database using the 'DROP INDEX' statement.

```
DROP INDEX employees_last_name_ix;
```

Conclusion

Creating and managing indexes in Oracle Database plays a significant role in improving query performance. Therefore, it's essential to understand how to create, view, alter, rebuild, and drop indexes based on the database performance concerns.

3.7 What are the different types of subqueries in SQL, and when would you use them?

A subquery is a query within another query, used to retrieve data needed for further analysis within a parent query. There are several types of subqueries in SQL, each with its own specific use cases:

1. Scalar Subquery: A scalar subquery is a subquery that returns a single value, which is used in parent query like any other column. Scalar subqueries are typically used for calculations within a SELECT statement or as a parameter for a function within a WHERE clause.

Example:

```
SELECT customer_name,
       (SELECT AVG(transaction_amount) FROM transactions WHERE customer_id =
            customers.id) AS average_transaction_amount
FROM customers;
```

2. Single Row Subquery: Single row subqueries return only a single row and are typically used to check for the existence of data or retrieve a single value to be compared with a value in the parent query.

Example:

```
SELECT customer_name
FROM customers
WHERE customer_id = (SELECT customer_id FROM transactions WHERE
     transaction_id = 12345);
```

3. Multiple Row Subquery: Multiple row subqueries return multiple rows, and are used to retrieve data from one or more tables based on a condition in the parent query.

Example:

```
SELECT customer_name
FROM customers
WHERE customer_id IN (SELECT customer_id FROM transactions WHERE
     transaction_amount > 1000);
```

4. Correlated Subquery: A correlated subquery is a subquery that references a column from a table in the parent query. Correlated subqueries are typically used to filter data based on conditions in another table or to perform calculations based on data in related tables.

Example:

```
SELECT customer_name,
       (SELECT COUNT(*) FROM transactions WHERE transactions.customer_id =
            customers.customer_id) AS transaction_count
FROM customers;
```

Overall, subqueries are a powerful tool in SQL that allow for complex data retrieval and manipulation, and understanding the different types of subqueries and their use cases can significantly improve query performance and accuracy.

3.8 Can you explain the concept of database normalization and the different normal forms?

Database normalization is a process that helps to minimize data redundancy and dependency in a database by breaking down large and complex databases into smaller, more manageable ones. Normalization ensures that information is stored in databases accurately and logically, preventing any duplication of data and inconsistencies.

There are different levels of normalization or normal forms, which include:

1. First Normal Form (1NF): The first normal form requires that there should be no repeating groups of data and that each column should have a unique name. For example, a table of customers should avoid having multiple columns for phone numbers, instead, have a separate phone number table.

2. Second Normal Form (2NF): The second normal form requires that every non-key attribute is fully dependent on the primary key. This means that a table with a composite primary key where some fields are not dependent on the primary key should be split into two separate tables.

3. Third Normal Form (3NF): The third normal form eliminates transitive dependencies, meaning that there should be no non-key attributes that depend on another attribute that is not part of the primary key. If a table contains data that can be derived from another table already in the database, it should be moved to that table instead.

4. Fourth Normal Form (4NF): The fourth normal form requires that a table does not contain multiple independent multi-valued facts about an entity. In other words, if a table contains combinations of data that can create multiple relationships and contradictions, it should be split into separate tables.

5. Fifth Normal Form (5NF) or Domain-Key Normal Form (DK/NF): The fifth normal form is the highest level of normalization, and it requires that a table does not contain any join dependencies or join

keys. It means that sometimes two tables may have the same relationship through an intermediate table, and this intermediate table should be eliminated.

Normalization helps to ensure data accuracy and consistency, speed up query processing times, and reduce data redundancy in the overall database. However, over-normalizing a database can also lead to performance problems, so it's important to strike a balance between normalization and performance optimization.

3.9   What are sequences in Oracle databases, and how can they be used for generating unique values?

In Oracle databases, a sequence is a database object that generates a series of unique values. A sequence is often used to provide a unique primary key value for a table.

To create a sequence, you can use the CREATE SEQUENCE statement. Here is an example:

```
CREATE SEQUENCE myseq
START WITH 1
INCREMENT BY 1;
```

This creates a sequence named 'myseq' that starts at 1 and increments by 1 for each value generated.

To use the sequence to generate a unique value, you can use the NEXTVAL function. Here is an example:

```
INSERT INTO mytable (id, name)
VALUES (myseq.NEXTVAL, 'John');
```

This inserts a new row into 'mytable' with a unique ID value generated by the 'myseq' sequence.

Sequences can also be customized further by specifying minvalue, maxvalue, cycle/no cycle options, cache/no cache option, etc. Moreover, different sequences can be created in different schemas, each with its own characteristics.

In summary, sequences are useful for generating unique values and ensuring that there are no duplicate values in a table's primary key column.

3.10   What is the purpose of the Oracle System Global Area (SGA), and what are its main components?

The Oracle System Global Area (SGA) is a shared memory region in Oracle Database that contains data and control information for the database instance. It is used to improve database performance by reducing the amount of physical I/O operations that are required to access data, and by enabling efficient sharing of data between database sessions.

The SGA is divided into several components, each of which serves a specific purpose. The main components of the SGA are:

1. Buffer Cache: This component is responsible for caching frequently accessed data blocks from datafiles. When a user process requests data, Oracle first checks if the data block is available in the buffer cache. If it is, the data is returned from the buffer cache. If it is not, the data block is retrieved from disk and added to the cache.

2. Shared Pool: This component is used by Oracle to cache frequently used SQL statements, parsed statements or execution plans, PL/SQL procedures, function calls, shared cursors, and other data structures to share them across multiple database sessions. The shared pool also contains the library cache, which stores information about database objects required by SQL and PL/SQL statements.

3. Redo Log Buffer: This component is used to store information about changes made to the database, such as insert, update, and delete operations. This information is written to the redo log files to ensure that the database can be recovered in the event of a system failure.

4. Large Pool: This component is used to allocate memory for large memory allocations for certain operations like backup, recovery, and

Parallel Execution Server.

5. Java Pool: This component is used to store session-specific Java objects and metadata for Java Virtual Machine.

6. Streams Pool: This component is used to hold streams pool buffers used for Oracle Streams technology.

Each component of the SGA is allocated according to the initialization parameters specified in the instance startup parameter file. These parameters determine the sizes and configurations of individual SGA components.

In summary, the SGA plays an important role in Oracle Database performance by improving system efficiency and reducing I/O operations required to access frequently used data. The various components of the SGA work together to ensure efficient memory allocation and data sharing across the database.

3.11   Can you explain the concept of table partitioning in Oracle databases and its advantages?

Oracle Table Partitioning is a feature offered by Oracle Database that allows you to decompose a large table into smaller and more manageable pieces called partitions. Each partition is treated as a separate unit, and the data within each partition is stored separately from the rest of the table. This can result in significant improvement in query performance, as selective queries can now scan only relevant partitions rather than the entire table.

Partitioning can be defined based on a range of values, such as date or integer ranges, or based on a list of discrete values such as regions or departments. Additionally, partitioning can also be defined based on the hash value of a column or a combination of columns.

Partitioning a table can have various benefits, such as:

1. Improved query performance: Partitioning allows queries to be

executed on a subset of data, avoiding the need to scan the entire
table. This can result in faster query response times.

2. Easier data management: Partitioning allows you to quickly add
or remove data from a table partition, making it more manageable.
For example, in a sales table partitioned by region, you can easily add
new regions to the table without affecting existing regions.

3. Easier maintenance: Partitioning allows you to perform maintenance operations on specific partitions rather than the entire table,
minimizing downtime and reducing the impact of maintenance activities on the system.

4. Better data availability: Partitioning can be used in conjunction
with other Oracle features, such as Materialized Views and Advanced
Replication, to improve data availability and redundancy.

For example, the following code creates a range partitioned table with
four partitions, partitioned by the hire_date column:

```
CREATE TABLE employees (
  emp_id  NUMBER,
  last_name VARCHAR2(50),
  hire_date DATE
)
PARTITION BY RANGE (hire_date)
(
  PARTITION p1 VALUES LESS THAN (TO_DATE('01-JAN-2000', 'DD-MON-YYYY')),
  PARTITION p2 VALUES LESS THAN (TO_DATE('01-JAN-2005', 'DD-MON-YYYY')),
  PARTITION p3 VALUES LESS THAN (TO_DATE('01-JAN-2010', 'DD-MON-YYYY')),
  PARTITION p4 VALUES LESS THAN (MAXVALUE)
);
```

In this example, the table is partitioned into four partitions based
on the hire_date column. Partition p1 will contain records with hire
date less than Jan 1, 2000, partition p2 will contain records with hire
date less than Jan 1, 2005, and so on. All records with hire date
greater than or equal to Jan 1, 2010 will be stored in partition p4.

Overall, table partitioning is a powerful feature that can significantly
improve performance, manageability, and availability of large tables.

3.12 What are the different types of PL/SQL blocks, and how do they differ?

PL/SQL (Programming Language/Structured Query Language) is a powerful and efficient programming language that can be used to interact with Oracle databases. PL/SQL blocks are sections of PL/SQL code that can be executed together, and different types of PL/SQL blocks serve different purposes.

The different types of PL/SQL blocks are:

1. Anonymous PL/SQL blocks - These are standalone PL/SQL blocks that can be executed once. They do not have a name and cannot be called from other programs. Anonymous blocks can be useful for testing or for performing simple operations.

Example:

```
BEGIN
  DBMS_OUTPUT.PUT_LINE('Hello, World!');
END;
```

2. Stored procedures - Stored procedures are named PL/SQL blocks that can be called from other programs or scripts. They are stored in the database and can be reused as many times as needed. Stored procedures can accept input parameters and can also return values.

Example:

```
CREATE OR REPLACE PROCEDURE get_employee_details (
  p_employee_id IN NUMBER,
  p_name        OUT VARCHAR2,
  p_salary      OUT NUMBER
)
AS
BEGIN
  SELECT first_name || ' ' || last_name, salary
  INTO  p_name, p_salary
  FROM  employees
  WHERE employee_id = p_employee_id;
END;
```

3. Stored functions - Stored functions are similar to stored procedures, but they always return a value. Stored functions can be called from other programs or scripts and can be used in SQL statements.

Example:

```
CREATE OR REPLACE FUNCTION calculate_bonus (p_salary IN NUMBER)
RETURN NUMBER
AS
  bonus NUMBER;
BEGIN
  IF p_salary > 10000 THEN
    bonus := p_salary * 0.1;
  ELSE
    bonus := p_salary * 0.05;
  END IF;
  RETURN bonus;
END;
```

4. Packages - Packages are collections of related functions, procedures, and other constructs that can be stored in the database and reused by other programs or scripts. Packages provide a higher level of encapsulation and organization than standalone functions or procedures.

Example:

```
CREATE OR REPLACE PACKAGE employee_mgmt AS
  FUNCTION get_employee_name (p_employee_id IN NUMBER) RETURN VARCHAR2;
  PROCEDURE update_employee_salary (p_employee_id IN NUMBER, p_new_salary IN
      NUMBER);
END;
/
CREATE OR REPLACE PACKAGE BODY employee_mgmt AS
  FUNCTION get_employee_name (p_employee_id IN NUMBER) RETURN VARCHAR2
  AS
    name VARCHAR2(100);
  BEGIN
    SELECT first_name || '␣' || last_name
    INTO  name
    FROM  employees
    WHERE employee_id = p_employee_id;
    RETURN name;
  END;

  PROCEDURE update_employee_salary (p_employee_id IN NUMBER, p_new_salary IN
      NUMBER)
  AS
  BEGIN
    UPDATE employees
    SET    salary = p_new_salary
    WHERE employee_id = p_employee_id;
  END;
END;
```

In summary, PL/SQL blocks come in several different types, each with its own set of specific features and intended use. Understanding the different PL/SQL block types is crucial for designing efficient and effective database programs that can quickly and accurately retrieve, manipulate, and store data.

3.13   What are the primary differences between functions and procedures in PL/SQL?

In PL/SQL, functions and procedures are used to create modularized and reusable code blocks. Although the two are similar in many ways, they have some primary differences which are as follows:

1. Return Value: A function always returns a value whereas a procedure may or may not return a value. A function is required to contain a "RETURN" statement to specify the return value. The return value of a procedure is represented by an OUT parameter.

Example of a function with a return value:

```
CREATE FUNCTION get_employee_name (id NUMBER)
RETURN VARCHAR2
IS
  e_name VARCHAR2(100);
BEGIN
  SELECT name INTO e_name FROM employees WHERE employee_id = id;
  RETURN e_name;
END;
```

2. Usage: Functions are used to compute and return a single value whereas procedures are used to perform an action and manipulate the data in the database. Functions can be used in SQL queries, inside expressions and can be assigned to variables. Procedures perform database operations, but they do not return any value.

Example procedure:

```
CREATE PROCEDURE delete_employee (id NUMBER)
IS
BEGIN
  DELETE FROM employees WHERE employee_id = id;
END;
```

3. Constraints: Functions are allowed to be used in SQL statements and are subject to various constraints such as not allowing DML operations inside them. Whereas, procedures are not subject to these constraints and can contain DML inside them.

4. Calling conventions: Procedures can be called from other procedures, functions or directly from the SQL environment. Functions can

also be called from procedures and functions but cannot be called from SQL statements that modify data (INSERT, UPDATE, DELETE).

Example function call:

```
DECLARE
  emp_name VARCHAR2(100);
BEGIN
  emp_name := get_employee_name(101);
END;
```

3.14 How do you use exception handling in PL/SQL to manage errors?

In PL/SQL, exception handling is used to manage errors that may occur during the execution of a program. Exception handling involves identifying the type of error that occurred and taking appropriate actions to handle the error.

In order to use exception handling in PL/SQL, you need to define one or more exception handlers in your program. An exception handler is a block of code that is executed when a particular exception is raised. The general syntax for defining an exception handler is as follows:

```
BEGIN
  -- Some code here
EXCEPTION
  WHEN exception1 THEN
    -- Code to handle exception1
  WHEN exception2 THEN
    -- Code to handle exception2
  WHEN others THEN
    -- Code to handle all other exceptions
END;
```

In this syntax, 'exception1' and 'exception2' are specific exception names, and 'others' is a special exception name that handles all exceptions that are not caught by other handlers. Within each exception handler block, you can include code to handle the specific exception that has been raised.

Here's an example of how you might use exception handling in PL/SQL:

```
DECLARE
  balance NUMBER := 1000;
  withdrawal_amount NUMBER := 2000;
```

```
BEGIN
   IF withdrawal_amount > balance THEN
      RAISE_APPLICATION_ERROR(-20001, 'Insufficient␣funds');
   ELSE
      balance := balance - withdrawal_amount;
   END IF;
EXCEPTION
   WHEN OTHERS THEN
      DBMS_OUTPUT.PUT_LINE(SQLERRM);
END;
```

In this example, we have a 'balance' variable that starts at 1000 and
a 'withdrawal_amount' variable that is set to 2000. We check to see
if the withdrawal amount is greater than the balance, and if it is, we
raise an application error using the 'RAISE_APPLICATION_ER-
ROR' procedure. This will cause the program to jump to the exception handler block and execute the 'DBMS_OUTPUT.PUT_LINE
(SQLERRM)' statement, which will display the error message associated with the exception.

In summary, exception handling in PL/SQL involves defining one or
more exception handler blocks to handle specific types of errors that
may occur during program execution. By using exception handling,
you can create more robust and error-tolerant programs that can
gracefully handle unexpected situations.

3.15   What is the difference between a correlated and a non-correlated subquery?

A subquery is a query that is nested inside another query, usually en-
closed in parentheses. It can be either a correlated or a non-correlated
subquery.

A non-correlated subquery is a subquery that can be executed independently of the outer query. It is evaluated only once and the result
is used as a fixed value for the outer query. In other words, the subquery is not related to the outer query, and it can be executed on its
own. Here's an example:

```
SELECT name
FROM customers
WHERE age > (SELECT AVG(age) FROM customers);
```

The subquery '(SELECT AVG(age) FROM customers)' returns a single value, which is then used to filter the results of the outer query. This subquery is not correlated to the outer query, which means it can be executed independently of it.

On the other hand, a correlated subquery is a subquery that is related to the outer query. In other words, the subquery is executed once for each row of the outer query. The result of the subquery depends on the values of the outer query. Here's an example:

```
SELECT name, (SELECT COUNT(*) FROM orders WHERE customer_id = customers.id)
    AS order_count
FROM customers;
```

In this query, the subquery '(SELECT COUNT(*) FROM orders WHERE customer_id = customers.id)' depends on the value of 'customers.id' in the outer query. For each row in the outer query, the subquery is executed with a different value of 'customers.id'. This is called correlation. It means that the subquery is executed once for each row of the outer query, which can make correlated subqueries slower than non-correlated subqueries.

To summarize, the main difference between correlated and non-correlated subqueries is whether or not they are related to the outer query. Non-correlated subqueries can be evaluated independently of the outer query, while correlated subqueries are executed once for each row of the outer query.

3.16 Can you explain the process of using the Oracle Data Pump for exporting and importing data?

Oracle Data Pump is a powerful utility tool that allows you to export and import data and metadata between Oracle databases.

1. Exporting data with Oracle Data Pump
To export data, you start by creating an export job using the 'expdp' command. This command requires several parameters to be specified, such as the Oracle database schema to be exported, the directory object that identifies where the data pump files will be written, and

the full path file name to which the dump file set will be written.
Here is an example command line:

```
expdp schema_name DIRECTORY=data_pump_dir DUMPFILE=schema_name_exp.dmp
```

This command exports the entire schema named 'schema_name' and
writes the dump file to the directory object 'data_pump_dir' with
the file name 'schema_name_exp.dmp'. The 'expdp' command also
allows you to specify numerous other parameters, such as table filtering options, network link encryption, and compression options.

2. Importing data with Oracle Data Pump
After you have created an export job and generated a dump file set,
you can import the data into a new or existing database schema using
the 'impdp' command. This command requires several parameters
to be specified as well, such as the Oracle database schema to be
imported into, the directory object that identifies where the dump
file set is located, and full path file name from which the dump file
set is read. Here is an example command line:

```
impdp schema_name DIRECTORY=data_pump_dir DUMPFILE=schema_name_exp.dmp
```

This command imports the entire schema named 'schema_name' and
retrieves the dump file from the directory object 'data_pump_dir'
with the file name 'schema_name_exp.dmp'. The 'impdp' command
also allows you to specify numerous other parameters such as tablespace mapping options, object remapping options, and network
link encryption options.

3. Benefits of using Oracle Data Pump
Oracle Data Pump offers several advantages over traditional Oracle
Export and Import utilities. One of the key advantages is the ability
to specify the name of the destination tablespace while importing data
- this allows different tablespaces to be used for different modules of
the application, making it easier to manage data files and locate data
files for specific objects. Additionally, Oracle Data Pump is much
more efficient when it comes to exporting and importing large data
sets. This is mainly due to the use of parallelism which allows Data
Pump to use multiple worker processes to improve the speed of the
transfer.

Overall, Oracle Data Pump is an essential tool for any Oracle database
administrator as it makes exporting and importing Oracle Data be-

tween databases much easier and more efficient.

3.17 How can you monitor and improve the performance of SQL queries in an Oracle database?

Monitoring and improving the performance of SQL queries in an Oracle database is crucial to ensure optimal performance and efficient use of database resources. There are several ways to monitor and improve the performance of SQL queries in an Oracle database:

1. Use SQL Tracing: SQL tracing is a powerful tool that allows you to monitor the execution of SQL statements in real-time. Tracing helps to identify the inefficient queries, tuning the SQL queries and improving the performance. SQL tracing generates a trace file that contains detailed information about the execution of a SQL statement, including its execution plan, execution time, and other statistics.

To enable SQL tracing for a particular SQL statement, you can use the following command:

```
ALTER SESSION SET SQL_TRACE = TRUE;
```

To disable SQL tracing, you can use the following command:

```
ALTER SESSION SET SQL_TRACE = FALSE;
```

2. Use SQL Tuning Advisor: SQL Tuning Advisor is an Oracle Database feature that helps to identify the inefficient SQL statements and provides recommendations on how to improve their performance. It uses Automatic SQL Tuning to run diagnostic checks, analyze the SQL statements, and suggest optimized SQL profiles.

To use the SQL Tuning Advisor, you can use the following command:

```
EXEC DBMS_SQLTUNE.CREATE_TUNING_TASK (SQL_ID => 'xxxxxx', SCOPE =>
    DBMS_SQLTUNE.SCOPE_COMPUTE);
```

This command creates a new SQL tuning task for the SQL statement identified by the SQL_ID 'xxxxxx'. After creating the tuning task, you can run it using the following command:

```
EXEC DBMS_SQLTUNE.EXECUTE_TUNING_TASK(TASK_NAME => 'task_name');
```

This command executes the tuning task that you created earlier. The results of the tuning task are stored in the database as SQL profiles that can be implemented to improve the SQL query's performance.

3. Analyze Database Performance: Oracle Database provides several tools for analyzing database performance, including Oracle Enterprise Manager and Automatic Workload Repository (AWR). These tools analyze the performance of the database and identify bottlenecks and performance issues.

To use Oracle Enterprise Manager, you can log in to the Enterprise Manager console and select the Database Performance option. This option provides a graphical representation of the database performance, including the CPU usage, memory usage, and database wait time.

To use Automatic Workload Repository (AWR), you can create an AWR report that provides detailed information on the performance of the database. To create an AWR report, you can use the following command:

```
SELECT dbms_workload_repository.awr_report_text(snap_id1, snap_id2, dbid) AS
    report
FROM dba_hist_snapshot
WHERE snap_id1 = &snapid1
AND snap_id2 = &snapid2;
```

This command creates an AWR report for the specified snapshot IDs and database ID.

In conclusion, monitoring and improving the performance of SQL queries in an Oracle database is critical to ensure optimal database performance. By using SQL tracing, SQL Tuning Advisor, and database performance analysis tools, you can identify the inefficient SQL statements, optimize their execution, and improve overall database performance.

3.18 What is the role of the Oracle Redo Log, and how does it relate to database recovery?

The Oracle Redo Log is a fundamental component of an Oracle database that plays a crucial role in maintaining data consistency and ensuring database recovery.

At a high level, the Redo Log is a set of files that record all changes made to the database. Whenever a transaction modifies data in the database, the corresponding changes are written to the Redo Log files. The purpose of this is two-fold:

1. **Data recovery**: If the database experiences a failure, such as a power outage or hardware failure, the Redo Log files can be used to bring the database back to a consistent state. By applying the changes recorded in the Redo Log, the database can be replayed to the point in time just before the failure occurred. This allows the database to recover any changes that were not yet written to disk at the time of the failure.

2. **Data replication**: In addition to serving as a tool for recovery, the Redo Log is also used as part of Oracle's replication and standby database technologies. By shipping the Redo Log files to a secondary database, changes made to the primary database can be replicated to the secondary database in near-real time.

Technically speaking, the Redo Log is a circular buffer that is stored in memory. Whenever a transaction modifies data in the database, the corresponding changes are recorded in the Redo Log buffer. Periodically, the contents of the buffer are flushed to disk in the form of Redo Log files.

During a recovery scenario, the Redo Log files are used in conjunction with the database's datafiles to bring the database back to a consistent state. The basic process works as follows:

```
1. Identify the most recent Redo Log file that has been written to disk
2. Determine which changes were made to the database in that Redo Log file
3. Reapply those changes to the database's␣datafiles,␣bringing␣the␣database␣
   back␣to␣a␣consistent␣state
```

This process is repeated for each Redo Log file until the database is caught up to the point in time just before the failure occurred.

In summary, the Oracle Redo Log is a critical component of Oracle's database architecture. It helps to ensure data consistency and enables fast recovery in the event of a failure. By continuously recording all changes made to the database, the Redo Log allows the database to recover any changes that were not yet written to disk at the time of a failure. Ultimately, this helps to ensure that your data is always available and up-to-date.

3.19   What are the different types of database links in Oracle, and how do they work?

There are several types of database links in Oracle:

1. Private database link: This type of database link is created and owned by a specific user and is visible only to that user. It can be used to access objects in another database that the user has permission to access.

2. Public database link: This type of database link is created and owned by a database administrator (DBA) and is visible to all users in the database. It can be used by any user to access objects in the remote database that the DBA has granted permission to access.

3. Global database link: This type of database link is created and owned by a database administrator and is visible to all users in all databases in the same network. It can be used to access objects in a remote database that the DBA has granted permission to access.

4. Shared database link: This type of database link is created and owned by a specific user, but is made available to other users in the same database. It can be used to access objects in a remote database that the user has permission to access.

Database links work by creating a connection between two databases, allowing objects in one database to be accessed from the other database. When a query or transaction is issued that references an object in a remote database, the local database uses the database link to establish a connection to the remote database and retrieves the necessary data.

For example, let's say we have two databases: DB1 and DB2. We want to access a table called "customers" in DB2 from DB1. We can create a public database link in DB1 that connects to DB2 and grants access to the "customers" table. Then, when we issue a query in DB1 that references the "customers" table, the local database will use the public database link to establish a connection to DB2 and retrieve the necessary data.

Here's an example of creating a database link in Oracle:

```
CREATE DATABASE LINK db2_link CONNECT TO db2_user IDENTIFIED BY password
    USING 'db2_tns';
```

This creates a database link called "db2_link" that connects to a remote database using the "db2_tns" service name, and authenticates using the username "db2_user" and password "password".

Once the database link is created, we can use it to access remote objects in our queries and transactions, like this:

```
SELECT * FROM customers@db2_link;
```

This retrieves all rows from the "customers" table in the remote database connected by the "db2_link" database link.

3.20   How can you schedule and manage jobs in Oracle databases using the DBMS_SCHEDULER package?

The DBM_SCHEDULER package in Oracle databases provides a powerful tool for scheduling and managing jobs. With this package, users can schedule jobs to run at specific times or intervals, monitor and manage job status, and even create job chains to ensure that dependent jobs run in the correct order.

To get started with DBMS_SCHEDULER, the first step is to create a job definition. This can be done using the CREATE_JOB procedure, which takes a number of input parameters including the job name, the program to run, and the schedule interval.

For example, to create a job that runs every day at noon, we could use the following code:

```
BEGIN
  DBMS_SCHEDULER.CREATE_JOB (
    job_name        => 'daily_job',
    program_name    => 'my_program',
    start_date      => SYSTIMESTAMP,
    repeat_interval => 'FREQ=DAILY;BYHOUR=12;',
    enabled         => TRUE);
END;
/
```

Once the job definition is in place, we can use the ENABLE procedure to start the job running. We can also use the DISABLE procedure to temporarily pause a job, or the DROP_JOB procedure to remove it entirely.

To monitor the status of a job, we can use the JOB_RUN_DETAILS view, which provides information about past and current runs of the job. We can also use the SET_ATTRIBUTE and GET_AT-TRIBUTE procedures to set and retrieve job attributes, such as the logging level or maximum run time.

One powerful feature of DBMS_SCHEDULER is the ability to create job chains, which allow dependent jobs to be run in a specific order. For example, we could create a job chain with three jobs:

```
BEGIN
  DBMS_SCHEDULER.CREATE_JOB (
    job_name        => 'job1',
    program_name    => 'program1',
    enabled         => TRUE);

  DBMS_SCHEDULER.CREATE_JOB (
    job_name        => 'job2',
    program_name    => 'program2',
    enabled         => TRUE);

  DBMS_SCHEDULER.CREATE_JOB (
    job_name        => 'job3',
    program_name    => 'program3',
    enabled         => TRUE);

  DBMS_SCHEDULER.CREATE_CHAIN (
    chain_name      => 'my_chain',
    rule_set_name   => NULL,
    evaluation_interval=> NULL,
    comments        => 'My Job Chain');

  DBMS_SCHEDULER.DEFINE_CHAIN_STEP (
    chain_name      => 'my_chain',
    step_name       => 'step1',
```

```
    job_name         => 'job1');

 DBMS_SCHEDULER.DEFINE_CHAIN_STEP (
    chain_name       => 'my_chain',
    step_name        => 'step2',
    job_name         => 'job2');

 DBMS_SCHEDULER.DEFINE_CHAIN_STEP (
    chain_name       => 'my_chain',
    step_name        => 'step3',
    job_name         => 'job3');

 DBMS_SCHEDULER.START_CHAIN (
    chain_name       => 'my_chain');
END;
/
```

In this example, job1 must run successfully before job2 can start, and job2 must run successfully before job3 can start.

Overall, the DBMS_SCHEDULER package in Oracle databases provides a robust tool for scheduling and managing jobs. By using job definitions, job chains, and related functions, users can ensure that tasks are executed on time and in the correct order.

Chapter 4

Advanced

4.1 What is the difference between a star schema and a snowflake schema in data warehousing, and when would you use each?

In data warehousing, a schema is a logical structure that represents how data is organized in tables within a database. Star schema and snowflake schema are two different data modeling techniques used in data warehousing.

A star schema is a centralized schema where one or more fact tables are connected to multiple dimension tables. The fact table contains the measures or numerical data, while the dimension tables contain attributes that describe the data in the fact table. The relationship between the fact table and dimension tables is a one-to-many relationship, with the fact table acting as the center of the schema.

On the other hand, a snowflake schema is a more normalized schema where dimension tables are normalized into sub-dimension tables. This means that each dimension table is further divided into multiple sub-dimension tables for more granular information. These sub-dimension tables are connected to each other, forming a snowflake-like structure. This leads to more complex joins between dimension tables, but it allows for more flexibility and better data integrity.

The decision to use a star schema or a snowflake schema depends on the nature and complexity of the data being stored. A star schema is typically used for simple, straightforward queries where performance is critical. Since the schema is denormalized, it is easier and faster to query the data.

A snowflake schema, on the other hand, is best suited for more complex data where more detailed information is needed. Since the schema is normalized, it can handle more dimensions and provides better data integrity. However, this comes at the cost of more complex data joins, which can lead to slower query performance.

To illustrate the difference between the two schemas, consider an e-commerce website that wants to track the number of items sold and the total revenue generated by each product category. In a star schema, the fact table would contain the sales data, while the dimension tables would be product and category tables. The relationship between the fact table and the dimension tables would be a one-to-many relationship.

In a snowflake schema, the dimension table would be normalized. For example, the category table might be further divided into sub-dimension tables for sub-categories, and the product table might be further divided into sub-dimension tables for product features. This creates a more complex schema but allows for more detailed analysis of the data.

In summary, the choice between star schema and snowflake schema depends on the complexity of the data and the level of detail required for analysis. A star schema is simpler and faster for straightforward queries, while a snowflake schema is more complex but provides better data integrity and more detailed analysis capabilities.

4.2 How do you use Oracle's Materialized Views for query optimization, and what are their benefits?

Oracle's Materialized Views (MVs) are precomputed tables that store the results of a query, which can be refreshed periodically, on-demand, or based on specific events. They are useful in optimizing long-running and complex queries, especially those involving large datasets, by precomputing and storing the query results. In this way, MVs eliminate the need for repeated querying and computation on the original data source, leading to faster query response times and reduced database load.

Here are some of the benefits of using Materialized Views in Oracle:

1. Improved Query Performance: By precomputing and storing query results, MVs can perform complex queries more efficiently and can provide faster response times. In some cases, the use of MVs can eliminate the need for live table joins and complex SQL statements.

2. Reduced Database Load: Since MVs store precomputed results, they can reduce the load on the underlying base tables and databases. Queries that require complex joins, filtering, and aggregations on large tables can be addressed through MVs rather than having the database execute these queries repeatedly.

3. Simplified Reporting: MVs can be used for reporting and data warehousing, providing a simplified view of the data required for these processes. As businesses scale and require more detailed reports, MVs can help to aggregate data from different databases, making it easier to create real-time reports.

4. Reduced Network Traffic: MVs can be used to reduce network traffic between database nodes or systems. For example, a remote sales office could use MVs to access precomputed summary data for different products or regions.

To create an MV in Oracle, you can use the CREATE MATERIALIZED VIEW command. An example syntax for creating a simple MV would be:

```
CREATE MATERIALIZED VIEW mv_sales_report AS
SELECT product_name, sum(sales_amount) as total_sales,
       count(sales_id) as total_orders, month(sales_date) as sales_month
FROM sales_transactions
GROUP BY product_name, month(sales_date);
```

In this example, the query aggregates sales data from the sales_trans-
actions table by product and month, and computes the total sales
amount and number of orders for each combination. The resulting MV, mv_sales_report, will store the precomputed results of this
query and can be refreshed or queried on-demand.

To use the MV in a query, simply reference it like any other table:

```
SELECT product_name, total_orders, total_sales
FROM mv_sales_report
WHERE sales_month = 12;
```

In this example, the MV is queried to return sales data for the month
of December. The query execution time will be significantly faster
compared to querying the sales_transactions table directly, especially
if the source table has millions of rows.

In summary, Materialized Views can be used to precompute complex queries and improve query performance, reduce database load,
simplify reporting, and reduce network traffic. Creating an MV involves defining the query to precompute and storing the results in a
table. These precomputed results can then be queried as if they were
a normal table.

4.3   Can you explain the different types of table partitioning techniques in Oracle databases and their use cases?

Table partitioning is a powerful feature in Oracle database that provides several benefits such as improved query and load performance,
ease of maintenance, and enhanced availability. Partitioning is the
process of dividing a large table into smaller and more manageable
pieces called partitions based on some criteria. Each partition can be
stored in a separate file or tablespace, and can be managed independently. In Oracle database, there are several types of table partition-

ing techniques available, each with its own unique characteristics and use cases.

1. Range Partitioning: Range partitioning is the most commonly used partitioning technique in Oracle. It involves partitioning a table based on a range of values in a specific column, typically a date or numeric value. For example, a table can be partitioned by date, with each partition holding data for a specific range of dates, such as all transactions for a specific month. Range partitioning is useful when dealing with large datasets that require fast and efficient data retrieval with queries based on date or numeric ranges.

2. List Partitioning: List partitioning involves partitioning a table based on specific values in a column. For example, a table can be partitioned based on the country column, with each partition holding data for a specific country. List partitioning is useful when a table contains discrete values that can be partitioned based on categories.

3. Hash Partitioning: Hash partitioning involves partitioning a table based on a hashing algorithm that distributes data evenly across partitions. The hash function used for partitioning is typically a built-in Oracle function, such as the MD5 algorithm. Hash partitioning is useful when data is not correlated with any specific column and a uniform distribution of data across all partitions is desired.

4. Composite Partitioning: Composite partitioning is a combination of two or more partitioning techniques. For example, a table can be range-partitioned by date, and each partition can be further list-partitioned based on a specific country. Composite partitioning is useful when dealing with complex datasets that require multiple levels of partitions to optimize performance.

5. Interval Partitioning: Interval partitioning is a variation of range partitioning, where new partitions are created automatically based on an interval value. For example, a table can be interval-partitioned by date, where a new partition is automatically created for every new month. Interval partitioning is useful when dealing with very large datasets that require regular data additions and deletions.

Overall, choosing the right partitioning technique depends on the specific requirements of the database and the data it stores. Careful consideration should be given to the data model, access patterns, and performance characteristics of the database to determine the most appropriate partitioning technique.

4.4 What is the role of tablespaces in Oracle databases, and how do they help manage storage allocation?

In Oracle databases, a tablespace is a logical storage container for the data that is stored in the database. Tablespaces are used to organize and manage the storage of database objects such as tables, indexes, and other schema objects.

The main purpose of using tablespaces is to provide a way to manage the allocation of storage space for the database. Tablespace management involves creating, altering, and dropping tablespaces, and allocating space within the tablespaces to the database objects.

Tablespaces can be created to store different types of data or to separate data for different applications or users. For example, you might create separate tablespaces to store application data, index data, temporary data, and undo data. This allows you to manage and optimize the storage requirements of each type of data separately, which can improve performance and manageability.

With tablespaces, you can allocate and manage storage space for database objects easily. You can control the amount of storage allocated to each tablespace and monitor the space utilization of each tablespace. In addition, tablespaces allow you to manage the storage of objects that are too large to fit into a single data file. By spreading data across multiple data files, you can manage disk space more efficiently.

Tablespaces allow you to use different storage characteristics for different types of data. For example, you can assign specific data files to a tablespace and specify the storage capacity and performance characteristics for that data file. You can also specify different storage parameters for different tablespaces, such as file size, autoextend mode, block size, and data file location.

Here is an example of how tablespace management can be useful in Oracle databases:

Suppose you are developing an application that stores a large amount of image data. You might create a separate tablespace specifically for this type of data, with the following characteristics:

```
- Large data files to store the image data
- High-performance storage devices to optimize retrieval speed
- Different backup and recovery characteristics than for other types of data
```

By creating a separate tablespace for the image data, you can manage the storage of this type of data separately from other types of data in the database. You can monitor the data storage utilization of the image tablespace to ensure that it has sufficient space available. You can also back up and recover the image data separately from other database objects to ensure that you can restore the image data quickly and efficiently.

4.5 How do you perform database tuning in Oracle, and what are some common tools and techniques?

Database tuning is an important process that aims to optimize the performance of a database. In Oracle, there are various tools and techniques available to perform database tuning. In this answer, we will discuss some common tools and techniques used in Oracle for database tuning.

1. SQL Trace: SQL Trace is a tool used to collect and analyze performance data. It allows a user to trace SQL statements and obtain statistics regarding its execution. SQL Trace can be enabled at the session or system level. To enable SQL Trace for a session, the user can use the following command:

```
ALTER SESSION SET SQL_TRACE = TRUE;
```

Once the session is completed, the trace file can be analyzed using various tools, such as TKPROF and Oracle Enterprise Manager.

2. EXPLAIN PLAN: EXPLAIN PLAN is a tool that displays the
execution plan for a SQL statement. It provides information about
the operations performed, the order of the operations, and the access
paths used. The execution plan can be obtained using the following
command:

```
EXPLAIN PLAN FOR <SQL Statement>;
```

The execution plan can be viewed using the following command:

```
SELECT * FROM TABLE(DBMS_XPLAN.DISPLAY());
```

The output from EXPLAIN PLAN can help identify potential bottlenecks in the SQL statement.

3. Oracle Enterprise Manager: Oracle Enterprise Manager is a web-
based tool used to monitor and manage Oracle databases. It provides a variety of performance monitoring and management features.
It can be used to perform database tuning and troubleshooting activities, such as identifying the top SQL statements that are causing
performance problems, setting up alerts for performance metrics, and
analyzing performance data.

4. Automatic Workload Repository (AWR): AWR is a tool used to
collect and store performance data over time. It is used to monitor
system-level performance and identify trends and patterns. AWR
data can be analyzed using various tools, such as Oracle Enterprise
Manager and AWR reports.

5. SQL Tuning Advisor: SQL Tuning Advisor is a tool used to analyze SQL statements and provide recommendations to improve performance. It analyzes the SQL statement and suggests improvements,
such as creating indexes, changing optimizer settings, or restructur-
ing the SQL statement. The SQL Tuning Advisor can be accessed
through Oracle Enterprise Manager or the SQL Developer interface.

In summary, Oracle provides a variety of tools and techniques to
perform database tuning. SQL Trace, EXPLAIN PLAN, Oracle Enterprise Manager, AWR, and SQL Tuning Advisor are some of the
commonly used tools and techniques. By using these tools and techniques, a user can identify performance bottlenecks and optimize the
performance of an Oracle database.

4.6 What are the main differences between RMAN (Recovery Manager) and traditional user-managed backup and recovery methods?

RMAN (Recovery Manager) and traditional user-managed backup and recovery methods have significant differences in their approach, control, and flexibility. The main differences between these two methods are explained below.

1. Control and Automation: User-managed backup and recovery involve manual processes, and the DBA must execute each step manually. On the other hand, RMAN is a highly automated backup and recovery tool that provides centralized control over backup and recovery operations. It automates entire backup and recovery operations and eliminates the need for manual intervention.

2. Backup and Recovery Optimization: RMAN provides several optimization techniques like backup multiplexing, backup set compression, and dual tape streams that cannot be achieved in user-managed backups. These optimizations significantly reduce backup time and the volume of backup data to be stored, which results in faster restore times.

3. Incremental Backups and Recovery: Another significant difference between RMAN and User-managed backups is the concept of incremental backups. With User-managed backups, DBA can only perform full backups, while with RMAN, incremental backups can be taken, reducing the backup size and time. While restoring the database, RMAN can stitch together different backups to recover the database to any point in time with minimal data loss.

4. Backup Validation: RMAN can perform a checksum check on the backup pieces, validating the backup after completion. In comparison, user-managed backup needs manual validation for the backups, increasing the possibility of data corruption or inconsistency in backup format.

5. Data Corruption Detection and Recovery: With user-managed backups, restoring a corrupt backup requires detective work and trial

and error based on timestamps to identify where data is corrupt. RMAN has in-built functionality to detect data block corruption, and it can recover data from the remaining blocks.

6. Backup Encryption: RMAN can encrypt backup data during transit and storage. In comparison, user-managed backups require third-party tools to encrypt backups, adding complexity and maintenance costs.

In conclusion, RMAN offers efficient, controlled, and optimized backup and recovery operations. It offers advanced functionality, which makes it the preferred choice for Oracle database backup and recovery. Also, using RMAN enables DBA to ensure database recoverability and meet the RTO/RPO (recovery point objective / recovery time objective) targets.

4.7   How can you manage and monitor an Oracle database's performance using Oracle Enterprise Manager (OEM)?

Oracle Enterprise Manager (OEM) provides a set of tools and utilities to manage and monitor the performance of an Oracle database. The following are the steps to manage and monitor an Oracle database's performance using OEM.

1. Login to OEM: Login to the Oracle Enterprise Manager using a web browser by navigating to the URL http://<hostname>:<port>/em (replace <hostname> with the host name or IP address where the OEM is installed and <port> with the port number of the OEM).

2. Navigate to Performance Monitoring: In the OEM home page, click on the "Targets" menu and select "Databases". Click on the database that you want to manage and monitor. In the database home page, click on the "Performance" tab.

3. View Performance Information: The performance tab shows summary information about the database performance, such as CPU usage, memory usage, I/O operations, and network usage. You can also view the historical performance data by clicking on the "History" sub-

tab. You can select different time periods to analyze the performance information.

4. View Top Activity: Click on the "Top Activity" sub-tab to view the top SQL statements that are consuming CPU, memory, or I/O resources. You can drill down to the SQL statements and view the execution plans to understand how the SQL is being executed.

5. View SQL Plan Baselines: Click on the "SQL Plan Baselines" sub-tab to view the SQL plan baselines for the SQL statements. SQL plan baselines capture the execution plans for the SQL statements that have been optimized by the database optimizer. You can manage the SQL plan baselines and activate the best plans.

6. View Advisors: Click on the "Advisors" sub-tab to view the different advisors available in OEM. Advisors provide recommendations to improve the database performance. For example, the SQL Tuning advisor provides recommendations to improve the performance of SQL statements.

7. Setup Alerts: Click on the "Alerts" sub-tab to set up alerts to be notified when the database performance degrades. You can set up alerts for various performance metrics, such as CPU usage, memory usage, or I/O operations. You can also set up custom thresholds to trigger alerts.

Overall, using OEM, you can manage and monitor the performance of your Oracle database and proactively identify and resolve performance problems.

4.8 What are the key features of Oracle Real Application Clusters (RAC), and how do they enhance database availability and scalability?

Oracle Real Application Clusters (RAC) is a feature of Oracle Database that allows multiple instances to access a single physical database, thereby providing a highly available and scalable database solution.

Some of the key features of RAC that enhance database availability and scalability include:

1. Clustered Architecture: RAC enables the database to be deployed in a clustered environment, where multiple servers are connected via a high-speed interconnect. This architecture provides high availability and scalability by allowing multiple instances to access the same database concurrently.

2. Shared Cache: RAC allows all nodes in the cluster to share the same database buffer cache. This enables data to be accessed more quickly, and results in improved performance and scalability.

3. Automatic Workload Management: RAC uses Automatic Workload Management (AWM) to balance the workload across all instances in the cluster. AWM dynamically adjusts database and application resources to ensure high performance and availability.

4. Online Patching: RAC enables patching and upgrades to be performed on individual nodes while the system remains online. This minimizes downtime and increases availability.

5. Oracle Global Data Services: Oracle Global Data Services (GDS) provides a single, unified view of databases configured in a RAC environment. GDS enables load balancing and failover across multiple databases, providing increased availability and scalability.

6. Load Balancing: RAC provides built-in load balancing for applications accessing the database. This ensures that requests are evenly distributed across all nodes in the cluster, preventing overloading of individual nodes.

7. Transparent Application Failover: RAC enables transparent application failover in the event of a node failure or other issue. This feature ensures that application connections are automatically redirected to available nodes, providing high availability and minimizing downtime.

Overall, Oracle Real Application Clusters provides a highly available and scalable database solution that can be deployed in a variety of configurations to meet the needs of any organization.

4.9   Can you explain the concept of Oracle's Automatic Storage Management (ASM) and its benefits?

Oracle's Automatic Storage Management (ASM) is a disk management solution for Oracle database environments that provides simplified administration, improved performance, and increased storage utilization. ASM is an integrated part of the Oracle database, starting from version 10g. It manages the storage of data files, control files, SPFILEs, redo log files, and archived log files, using disk groups that are created by combining the physical disks that are available on the system.

ASM offers several benefits to database administrators, including:

1. Simplified Administration: ASM simplifies the management of storage by reducing the complexity of traditional volume managers and file systems. It eliminates the need for manual file and volume management tasks, such as creating file systems, partitioning disks, and configuring volumes. With ASM, data files are stored in disk groups and managed at the disk group level by the ASM instance.

2. Improved Performance: ASM can improve the performance of Oracle databases by providing consistent and optimized I/O. It manages the layout of data in disk groups to reduce disk head seeks and maintain optimal disk usage. ASM can also rebalance the database's storage to ensure that the database's load is evenly balanced across all available disks.

3. Increased Storage Utilization: ASM can help database administrators make better use of available storage resources by reducing wasted space. ASM supports the use of variable-size extents, allowing it to use space more efficiently than traditional file systems. It also supports features such as compression and duplicate removal, which can help further reduce the amount of disk space used by the database.

Moreover, ASM also allows for dynamic online allocation and deallocation of storage as and when required by the database. This enables scaling the storage capacity of the database without interrupting its availability. Another benefit of ASM is its self-diagnosing and self-repairing capabilities. ASM monitors the health of the storage components and automatically relocates data from a failing disk to a healthy disk in the disk group to prevent data loss. Finally, since ASM is integrated with the Oracle Database, database administrators can use familiar database management tools, such as Oracle Enterprise Manager, to manage ASM.

In conclusion, Oracle's Automatic Storage Management offers several benefits to database administrators such as simplified administration, better performance, increased storage utilization, dynamic online allocation, and self-repairing capabilities, which make it a popular choice for managing the storage of Oracle databases.

4.10   What is the role of the Oracle UNDO tablespace, and how does it help manage data consistency and recovery?

The Oracle UNDO tablespace is a critical component of the database that plays a vital role in ensuring data consistency and facilitating data recovery in case of a failure or error. The UNDO tablespace is responsible for maintaining a record of all the changes made to the database during a transaction. These changes are stored in the form of undo records that contain the original data values before they were modified or deleted by a transaction.

When a user begins a transaction, Oracle writes undo data into the UNDO tablespace as a safeguard against failed or partially executed transactions. If the transaction is committed successfully, the undo data is no longer needed and can be purged from the UNDO tablespace. However, if the transaction is rolled back, the undo data is used to reverse the effects of the transaction and restore the database to its previous state.

The UNDO tablespace also plays a critical role in preventing data inconsistencies due to concurrent transactions. When multiple users concurrently access the same data, conflicts can arise where one user's changes may overwrite another user's changes. To prevent this, Oracle uses the UNDO tablespace to manage concurrency and ensure that each transaction has access to consistent and correct data values.

Finally, the UNDO tablespace also plays a crucial role in database recovery in case of a failure or error. When a database encounters a problem, such as a system crash or a power outage, the database's state may become corrupted, leaving transactions partially executed, and data in an inconsistent state. In such cases, the UNDO tablespace can be used to restore the database's previous state by rolling back incomplete transactions and reverting changed data to its original values.

In summary, the Oracle UNDO tablespace is a crucial component of the database management system that helps ensure data consistency, manage concurrency, and facilitate data recovery in case of a failure or error. Without the UNDO tablespace, the database would be much more vulnerable to data inconsistencies and much more challenging to recover in the event of a failure or error.

4.11   Can you describe the difference between a complete, an incomplete, and a point-in-time recovery in Oracle databases?

In Oracle databases, there are three forms of database recovery: complete, incomplete, and point-in-time recovery.

A complete recovery is used to restore a database to a consistent state, typically after a catastrophic failure, such as a disk failure or a major system crash. In such situations, you would need to restore the last backup of the database and then replay all archived and redo logs generated since the backup. To perform a complete recovery, the database must be shut down and restarted with the resetlogs option.

An incomplete recovery is used to recover the database to a specific point in time between two backups, typically in the event of a minor issue such as a user error or a corrupt data block. In such situations, you would restore the last backups of the database and then apply all archived and redo logs generated between that backup and the point in time where the error occurred. Unlike with complete recovery, the database is not opened with the resetlogs option when performing an incomplete recovery.

A point-in-time recovery is a type of incomplete recovery that recovers the database to a specific point in time, rather than a specific SCN (System Change Number). This type of recovery is often used to recover from human error or application errors that occurred at a specific point in time. For example, if a user accidentally deletes a table at 3:00 PM, we could perform a point-in-time recovery to return the database to its state at 2:59 PM. This type of recovery is similar to an incomplete recovery, but instead of specifying a log sequence number (LSN) or SCN to stop recovery, we specify a timestamp to stop applying logs.

In summary, complete recovery restores a database to a consistent state after a catastrophic failure, incomplete recovery is used to recover the database to a specific point in time between two backups, and point-in-time recovery recovers the database to a specific point in time, rather than a specific SCN.

4.12   What is the difference between a package and a library in PL/SQL, and when should each be used?

In PL/SQL, a package is a named collection of related procedures, functions, and other constructs, stored as a schema object in the database. On the other hand, a library is a collection of database objects that encapsulate code for reuse, but do not necessarily have a specific name or exist as a single entity like a package.

The main difference between a package and a library is that a package is a self-contained unit of code, with named procedures, functions, constants, and other constructs, whereas a library is a collection of separate database objects, such as procedures or functions, that can be referenced or invoked from other code.

Packages are especially useful for organizing and encapsulating related functionality in a modular and reusable way, and providing a public interface to that functionality. They can also be used for fine-grained access control, since you can grant privileges to execute a package or its specific procedures and functions, but not to access or modify its underlying data. Additionally, since packages can have state (i.e., package-level variables), they can store data between procedure or function calls, which can be useful in certain situations.

Libraries, on the other hand, are generally used to encapsulate common or reusable functionality that is not directly related to a specific application or module. For example, a library might contain a set of utility procedures or functions, or a set of procedures for interacting with a third-party API or web service. Libraries are typically used as building blocks for larger applications, and are often shared between multiple applications or modules. However, since libraries do not have a specific name or access control mechanism like packages, they are not as secure and can be more difficult to manage and maintain.

In general, when deciding whether to use a package or a library, it's important to consider the level of encapsulation and organization that your code requires. If you have a set of related procedures or functions that require fine-grained access control or need to maintain state between calls, you may want to use a package. On the other hand, if you have a set of utility procedures or functions that can be reused across multiple applications or modules, a library may be more appropriate.

4.13   How do you optimize PL/SQL code using bulk processing techniques like FORALL and BULK COLLECT?

PL/SQL is a procedural language used to perform manipulation and processing in the Oracle Database. It allows the creation of functions, procedures, triggers, and other database objects that can improve the performance of applications running within the database.

Bulk processing techniques such as FORALL and BULK COLLECT allow for efficient and fast processing of large volumes of data. Here are some ways to optimize PL/SQL code using these techniques:

1. Use BULK COLLECT to retrieve large data sets

Oracle Database retrieves data one row at a time and stores it in a buffer cache. This process can take a lot of time if there are multiple round trips between the database and the application. By using BULK COLLECT, Oracle retrieves multiple rows at a time, reducing the number of round trips and boosting performance.

Here's an example of how to use BULK COLLECT:

```
DECLARE
  TYPE t_emp_tab IS TABLE OF employees%ROWTYPE;
  l_emp_tab t_emp_tab;
BEGIN
  SELECT * BULK COLLECT INTO l_emp_tab FROM employees WHERE department_id =
      50;
END;
```

2. Use FORALL to perform DML operations on large data sets

FORALL allows for the execution of DML statements (INSERT, UP-DATE, DELETE) in bulk, reducing the overhead of executing multiple DML statements individually. FORALL executes the DML statements as a single unit of work, which can significantly reduce the time taken to perform a large number of DML operations.

Here's an example of how to use FORALL:

```
DECLARE
  TYPE t_emp_tab IS TABLE OF employees%ROWTYPE;
  l_emp_tab t_emp_tab;
BEGIN
  SELECT * BULK COLLECT INTO l_emp_tab FROM employees WHERE department_id =
      50;
  FORALL i IN 1..l_emp_tab.COUNT
    UPDATE employees SET salary = l_emp_tab(i).salary * 1.1 WHERE employee_id
        = l_emp_tab(i).employee_id;
END;
```

3. Use BULK COLLECT with FORALL for maximum efficiency

Using BULK COLLECT and FORALL together can provide the maximum possible performance improvements. By BULK COLLECTing the data and FORALLing the DML operations, you can minimize context switches and reduce the overhead of multiple round trips to the database.

Here's an example of how to use BULK COLLECT with FORALL:

```
DECLARE
  TYPE t_emp_tab IS TABLE OF employees%ROWTYPE;
  l_emp_tab t_emp_tab;
BEGIN
  SELECT * BULK COLLECT INTO l_emp_tab FROM employees WHERE department_id =
```

```
        50;
    FORALL i IN 1..l_emp_tab.COUNT
      UPDATE employees SET salary = l_emp_tab(i).salary * 1.1 WHERE employee_id
          = l_emp_tab(i).employee_id;
    END;
```

In conclusion, the use of bulk processing techniques such as FORALL and BULK COLLECT can significantly improve the performance of PL/SQL code. By minimizing context switches, reducing round trips to the database, and executing DML statements as a single unit of work, you can create more efficient and faster applications.

4.14   How can you use Oracle's analytic functions to perform advanced data manipulation and analysis?

Oracle's analytic functions provide powerful tools for performing advanced data manipulation and analysis. These functions allow you to calculate aggregate values across different groups of data, calculate running totals and moving averages, rank and assign row numbers, and perform many other complex calculations.

One of the most basic examples of analytic functions is the use of windowing clauses. These clauses can be used to specify a subset of rows within a result set, over which calculations are performed. For instance, imagine you have a table of sales data with the following columns: 'Product, Date, Region, Sales'. You can use an analytic function to calculate the total sales for each product, but only for the previous month:

```
SELECT Product, Date, Region, Sales,
SUM(Sales) OVER (PARTITION BY Product ORDER BY Date
          RANGE BETWEEN INTERVAL '1' MONTH PRECEDING AND INTERVAL '1' DAY
          PRECEDING) AS PrevMonthSales
FROM SalesData
```

Here, we use the 'SUM' function as an analytic function, and specify a windowing clause that partitions the data by product and orders the rows by date. The 'RANGE BETWEEN INTERVAL '1' MONTH PRECEDING AND INTERVAL '1' DAY PRECEDING' clause specifies that we only want to sum the sales for the previous month. The result set will contain all original columns, plus a new column called

'PrevMonthSales' that contains the total sales for each product for the previous month.

Another example is the use of ranking functions like 'RANK', 'DENSE_RANK', and 'ROW_NUMBER'. These functions can be used to assign a unique rank or row number to each row in a result set, based on one or more columns. For instance, imagine you have a table of employee data with columns 'FirstName, LastName, Department, Salary'. You can use an analytic function to assign a rank to each employee based on their salary within their department:

```
SELECT FirstName, LastName, Department, Salary,
RANK() OVER (PARTITION BY Department ORDER BY Salary DESC) AS DepartmentRank
FROM EmployeeData
```

Here, we use the 'RANK' function as an analytic function, and specify a windowing clause that partitions the data by department and orders the rows by salary in descending order. The result set will contain all original columns, plus a new column called 'DepartmentRank' that contains the rank of each employee within their department based on salary.

In addition to these examples, there are many other ways to use Oracle's analytic functions to perform advanced data manipulation and analysis. By understanding how to use these functions, you can gain powerful insights into your data and make more informed decisions.

4.15   What are the key features of Oracle Database Vault, and how does it help secure sensitive data?

Oracle Database Vault is an optional security feature for Oracle Database that provides additional security controls to restrict access to sensitive data by enforcing a separation-of-duty principle. It works by protecting against privileged users, such as database administrators, who may be able to access or manipulate sensitive data for malicious purposes.

Here are the key features of Oracle Database Vault and how they help secure sensitive data:

1. Realms: Oracle Database Vault allows administrators to define realms, which are sets of database objects that are protected by a specific security policy. This feature makes it possible to enforce fine-grained access controls for different types of data based on its sensitivity. For example, a realm could be created to protect sensitive financial data, such as credit card numbers or account balances, and only designated users would be given access to that realm.

2. Command rules: Oracle Database Vault provides command rules, which allow administrators to regulate the types of SQL commands that can be executed on a specific set of database objects. This feature allows database administrators to prevent malicious commands from being executed on sensitive data. For example, a command rule could be created to prevent a user from executing DELETE statements on a sensitive table.

3. Factors: Factors is a feature of Oracle Database Vault that permits the integration of authentication and authorization of database users with enterprise-level systems. Factors can integrate with Directory Authentication System or other third-party authentication systems, such as Active Directory, and it can be used to customize the inter- action of the database with authenticated and authorized clients. It can be used to enforce restrictions on them regarding the data they are allowed to view or modify within the database.

4. Privilege analysis: With privilege analysis, Oracle Database Vault allows administrators to identify unused privileges that could be re- voked or to identify conflicting privileges that could be leveraged to obtain unauthorized access to sensitive data. This feature helps en- sure that only the necessary access is granted to users and that they are not given more privileges than they need to do their job.

Overall, Oracle Database Vault is a powerful security feature that can be used to secure sensitive data by providing fine-grained access controls based on the security policies defined by administrators. By enforcing separation of duties and limiting access to sensitive data, Oracle Database Vault helps to reduce the risk of malicious activity and unauthorized access to sensitive data.

4.16   Can you explain the different types of database triggers in Oracle and their use cases?

Oracle Database provides three types of database triggers:

1. **Row triggers**: These are fired for each row affected by a DML statement (INSERT, UPDATE or DELETE). Row triggers are useful for enforcing complex business rules, data validation and referential integrity constraints.

2. **Statement triggers**: These are fired once for each DML statement. Statement triggers are useful for auditing changes to tables, generating summary reports and logging events.

3. **System Event triggers**: These are fired based on specific system events such as database startup, shutdown or instance startup. System event triggers are useful for managing the environment, automating administrative tasks and handling exceptional conditions.

Here are some examples of each type of trigger:

1. **Row Trigger Example**: Suppose we have a requirement to enforce a business rule that prevents an employee from earning more than their manager. We can implement this using a row trigger on the EMPLOYEES table as follows:

```
CREATE OR REPLACE TRIGGER CHECK_EMPLOYEE_SALARY
BEFORE INSERT OR UPDATE ON EMPLOYEES
FOR EACH ROW
DECLARE
  manager_salary NUMBER;
BEGIN
  SELECT SALARY INTO manager_salary
  FROM EMPLOYEES
  WHERE EMPLOYEE_ID = :NEW.MANAGER_ID;

  IF :NEW.SALARY > manager_salary THEN
    RAISE_APPLICATION_ERROR(-20201, 'Employee salary cannot be greater than
        their manager');
  END IF;
END;
```

This trigger fires before a new row is inserted or an existing row is updated in the EMPLOYEES table, and checks if the salary of the employee is greater than the salary of their manager. If it is, an error is raised and the transaction is rolled back.

2. **Statement Trigger Example**: Suppose we have a requirement
to log all changes made to the EMPLOYEES table. We can implement this using a statement trigger as follows:

```
CREATE OR REPLACE TRIGGER LOG_EMPLOYEE_CHANGES
AFTER INSERT OR UPDATE OR DELETE ON EMPLOYEES
DECLARE
  operation VARCHAR2(10);
  timestamp TIMESTAMP;
BEGIN
  timestamp := SYSTIMESTAMP;

  IF INSERTING THEN
    operation := 'INSERT';
  ELSIF UPDATING THEN
    operation := 'UPDATE';
  ELSIF DELETING THEN
    operation := 'DELETE';
  END IF;

  INSERT INTO EMPLOYEE_AUDIT (EMPLOYEE_ID, OPERATION, TIME_STAMP)
  VALUES (:OLD.EMPLOYEE_ID, operation, timestamp);

END;
```

This trigger fires after an insert, update or delete statement is executed on the EMPLOYEES table, and logs the operation, employee
ID and timestamp to an AUDIT table.

3. **System Event Trigger Example**: Suppose we have a requirement to startup a background job whenever the database is started.
We can implement this using a system event trigger as follows:

```
CREATE OR REPLACE TRIGGER START_BACKGROUND_JOB
AFTER STARTUP ON DATABASE
BEGIN
  DBMS_SCHEDULER.CREATE_JOB(
    job_name        => 'BG_JOB',
    job_type        => 'PLSQL_BLOCK',
    job_action      => 'BEGIN MY_PACKAGE.RUN_BACKGROUND_PROCESS; END;',
    start_date      => SYSTIMESTAMP,
    repeat_interval => 'FREQ=DAILY; INTERVAL=1',
    enabled         => TRUE
  );
END;
```

This trigger fires automatically whenever the database is started, and
starts a background job using the DBMS_SCHEDULER package.
The background job runs a PL/SQL block that executes a package
procedure called MY_PACKAGE.RUN_BACKGROUND_PROCESS,
once a day.

4.17   What are the main components of Oracle's Automatic Workload Repository (AWR), and how do they help with performance tuning?

The Automatic Workload Repository (AWR) is a collection of metadata that provides statistics on the various components of an Oracle database's workload. It is the primary source of performance data for Oracle databases, and it can be used to identify performance bottlenecks and track their impact over time. The AWR collects information on all aspects of the database server, including system statistics, operating system events, memory usage, CPU usage, I/O usage, and SQL statements.

The main components of the AWR are:

1. Snapshots: The AWR takes regular snapshots of the database activity, which stores the contents of the statistics of the database at that specific time. By default, a new snapshot is taken every hour, or every 15 minutes in case of high load. This information is stored in the database's data dictionary and provides a detailed picture of the database's resource usage over time.

2. Baselines: A baseline serves as a reference point to see how performance changes over time. DBAs can manually create baselines and compare the existing performance data to those baselines. A baseline creation can be a point-in-time creation, where it is created manually before and after the major changes to the database. Also, a repeating baseline can be created to capture the performance metrics at a given interval.

3. Reports: Reports provide both high-level and detailed views of the AWR data. AWR reports help in identifying the cause of the problem by making them easy to navigate, consume and understand. Oracle provides several tools to generate reports, including the AWR Report, ADDM (Automatic Database Diagnostic Monitor), and ASH Analytics reports.

The AWR helps to identify performance issues in a few ways:

1. Performance trend analysis: The data collected by the AWR allows a DBA to identify trends in the performance of the database performance. If performance has degraded over time, it may indicate that the database is not correctly sized, or application workload has been increased.

2. Identification of most time-consuming operations: The Oracle AWR report ranks the most time-consuming SQL queries so that DBAs can tune them to improve performance. The ranking includes details such as the total time spent, waits, reads, and executions.

3. Identification of problems: The AWR periodically runs ADDM [Automatic Diagnostic/Diagnosis Monitor], which analyzes the workload and provides feedback on the actions that caused performance problems.

In conclusion, the AWR is a critical tool for performance monitoring and troubleshooting in Oracle Database systems. It provides detailed information on database usage and performance, and allows for trend analysis and baseline comparisons to identify and resolve performance issues.

4.18   What is the purpose of Oracle's Flashback technology, and how can it be used for data recovery?

Oracle's Flashback technology is a set of features that provide an easy way to recover data in case of logical corruptions, user error or other data loss issues. Its purpose is to allow the Oracle database to be reverted back to a previous state before the data loss occurred. Using Flashback, it is possible to recover dropped tables, deleted rows or even the entire database to a previous state, without performing a full database restore from a backup.

Oracle Flashback works by creating and maintaining a set of historical views and metadata that can be used to query the state data at different points in time. These views and metadata are updated automatically as the data changes and can be used in conjunction with the Oracle SQL language to perform queries against the historical state data.

One of the main benefits of Flashback technology is that it reduces the time required to recover data compared to more traditional backup and recovery methods. With Flashback technology, the recovery time objective (RTO) and recovery point objective (RPO) are significantly reduced, which is especially important for mission-critical systems that require high availability.

To use Flashback technology for data recovery, there are several features that can be utilized:

Flashback Query: This feature enables the retrieval of a specific set of data that was present in the past at a specific moment in time. It can be useful to retrieve accidentally deleted rows or to revert changes to data against a specific time. The query is performed using AS OF, which is included in the SELECT statement.

Flashback Table: This feature allows you to recover a table or its contents to a previous state. You can use this feature to recover a dropped table or to recover a specific version of a table by specifying the timestamp or SCN at which to recover the table.

Flashback Drop: This feature enables the recovery of a dropped table or any other object that has been dropped. It provides an easy way to recover data that has been dropped accidentally or mistakenly.

Flashback Transaction: This feature allows you to recover a transaction or a set of transactions to a previous state. You can use this feature to recover from logical corruptions or user errors that have caused data loss.

In summary, using Oracle Flashback technology, it is possible to quickly recover data from logical corruptions, user errors or other data loss issues. The various features of Flashback technology provide a quick and easy way to recover data, which reduces the time required for data recovery and ensures high availability of the Oracle database.

4.19 How can you use Oracle Data Guard for database replication and disaster recovery?

Oracle Data Guard is a feature of the Oracle Database that provides a high availability solution for both planned and unplanned outages. It enables you to create and maintain one or more standby databases that are synchronized with the primary database. Data Guard can be used for database replication and disaster recovery.

To use Oracle Data Guard for database replication and disaster recovery, you need to do the following:

1. Set up a primary database: The primary database is the database that contains the original data. This database must be configured to archive its redo logs and send them to the standby database.

2. Set up a standby database: The standby database is a copy of the primary database that is continuously updated from the archived redo log files that are sent by the primary database.

3. Configure Data Guard: You need to set up Data Guard to manage the replication and synchronization process between the primary and standby databases. This includes defining the redo transport services and the database roles (primary or standby) for each database.

4. Test the configuration: Before using Data Guard for disaster recovery, you should test your configuration to ensure that it is working correctly.

5. Perform regular maintenance: To keep your Data Guard configuration in good condition, you should perform regular maintenance tasks such as monitoring the standby database, updating configurations and patching the databases.

Here is an example of how to create a physical standby database using Oracle Data Guard:

1. Set up the primary database for archive log mode:

```
ALTER DATABASE ARCHIVELOG;
```

2. Create a standby control file:

```
ALTER DATABASE CREATE STANDBY CONTROLFILE AS '/u01/app/oracle/oradata/
    standby_controlfile.ctl';
```

3. Copy the archived redo logs to the standby server and configure the standby database:

```
- Copy the database backup from the primary server to the standby server.
- Set up network connectivity between the primary and standby databases.
- Start the standby database instance.
- Configure the standby database.
```

4. Set up the Data Guard broker:

```
- Edit the Broker configuration file.
- Start the Data Guard broker.
- Add the primary and standby databases to the broker configuration.
```

5. Start the transport services:

```
- Start the redo transport services.
- Verify that the redo transport services are working correctly.
```

6. Verify that the standby database is synchronized with the primary database:

```
- Check the status of the standby database.
- Verify that the standby database is in sync with the primary database.
```

7. Test the Data Guard configuration using switchover/failover operations.

Oracle Data Guard provides a comprehensive disaster recovery solution that ensures high availability of your databases in the event of planned and unplanned outages. By following the steps above, you can create a reliable and effective Data Guard configuration for your database replication and disaster recovery needs.

4.20 What is the Oracle Multitenant Architecture, and how does it help manage multiple databases efficiently?

Oracle Multitenant Architecture is a database feature introduced in Oracle Database 12c, which allows the creation of a single, multitenant container database (CDB) that can host multiple pluggable databases (PDBs). It is designed to help organizations to efficiently manage multiple databases and optimize hardware and software resources.

In a traditional database architecture, each database runs independently, occupying separate disk and memory space. This leads to wastage of resources and an increased administrative overhead as each database must be individually managed and maintained. However, the Multitenant Architecture eliminates this issue, as a single CDB provides a consolidated environment, enabling multiple PDBs to share the same hardware and software resources.

One of the main benefits of the Multitenant Architecture is resource management. A CDB can be better optimized because it allows for the sharing of resources among PDBs. For example, a PDB can share a single SGA (system global area), reducing the amount of memory consumed by each database instance. Similarly, a PDB can share a single set of processes, reducing the CPU resources used.

Another benefit of the Multitenant Architecture is the ease of manageability. Each PDB can be managed individually or as a group, making it easier and faster to patch or upgrade databases. Additionally, the DBA can manage the CDB and all associated PDBs as a single entity, so database maintenance tasks can be centralized and automated.

Here is an example of how the Multitenant Architecture works:

Let's say you have three databases: Database A, Database B, and Database C. In a traditional architecture, each database runs independently with its own hardware and software resources.

However, with the Multitenant Architecture, you can create a CDB and multiple PDBs. In this example, we've created a CDB and three

PDBs: PDB A, PDB B, and PDB C. All three PDBs share the same hardware and software resources, which reduces resource utilization.

Each PDB can have its own schemas, users, and data, but can still share certain resources with the other PDBs. In this example, PDB A and PDB B both use the same SGA and shared pool, while PDB C has its own.

In conclusion, Oracle Multitenant Architecture is a powerful feature that provides efficient management of multiple databases. By creating a single, multitenant container database and multiple pluggable databases, organizations can easily manage their databases, optimize their resources, and realize the benefits of increased scalability and flexibility.

Chapter 5

Expert

5.1 How does the Oracle Cost-Based Optimizer (CBO) work, and what factors does it consider when optimizing SQL queries?

The Cost-Based Optimizer (CBO) is a significant feature of the Oracle Database Management System. It is a database optimization engine designed to determine the optimal execution plan for SQL statements. The CBO analyzes data dictionary statistics to determine the most efficient access paths to query data.

The CBO works by selecting the lowest cost plan among the many possible execution plans for a given SQL statement. When an SQL statement is submitted to the database for execution, the CBO generates multiple execution plans for the statement based on available indexes, table scans, and join methods. Each plan has a cost, which is an estimate of the resources consumed by a particular execution plan to produce the result set.

The optimizer decides on the most efficient execution plan using a cost-based algorithm. The cost is determined by combining various factors, including:

1. Access Method: The optimizer evaluates the available access paths, including full table scans, index scans, nested loops, etc. and chooses the one with the lowest cost.

2. Join Order: For SQL statements that involve multiple tables, the order in which the tables are joined can significantly affect the performance. The optimizer tries to find a join order that reduces the cost of executing the query.

3. Join Methods: The optimizer considers various join methods such as nested loops, hash joins, and sort-merge joins. It chooses the one with the lowest cost.

4. Data Volume and Data Distribution: The optimizer evaluates the number of rows accessed and processed by each operation, as well as the distribution of data across tables and partitions, to determine the most efficient execution plan.

5. System Statistics: The optimizer considers system statistics, such as CPU speed, disk speed, and network speed, to estimate the time required to execute each operation in the execution plan.

6. Object Statistics: The optimizer considers object statistics, such as the number of distinct values in a column, the average length of a column, and the number of nulls, to make more accurate cost-based decisions.

For example, suppose we have a table called "ORDER" with columns "ORDER_ID," "CUSTOMER_ID," and "ORDER_DATE." The CBO can generate an execution plan that includes using an index on "CUSTOMER_ID" to locate rows in the "ORDER" table that have a particular value for customer ID to minimize the amount of data accessed. The optimizer can also choose to access the "ORDER" table using a full table scan if the selectivity of the query is low or to use a join, hash join, etc., to improve the overall performance.

In conclusion, the Cost-Based Optimizer is a critical component of the Oracle database. It analyzes several factors such as access methods, join order, join methods, data volumes, system statistics, and object statistics to choose the most efficient execution plan for a given SQL query. This optimization improves performance and responsiveness of the database, making it handle more queries efficiently.

5.2 Can you explain the different types of parallelism in Oracle databases and their impact on performance?

Oracle database provides various methods of parallelism to improve performance, which are as follows:

1. Parallel Query: In this method, the processing of a SQL statement is divided into multiple smaller tasks that are executed concurrently by multiple CPUs or nodes. Each parallel query operation has a degree of parallelism, which indicates the number of parallel execution servers that will be used.

For example, consider a query to select all the customers from a large table:

```
SELECT * FROM customers;
```

If the table is large, the query can be parallelized to improve the response time:

```
SELECT /*+ parallel(customers, 4) */ * FROM customers;
```

In this example, we are using parallel query with a degree of parallelism of 4. This means that the query will be divided into 4 smaller tasks and each task will be executed by a separate parallel execution server.

The impact of parallel query on performance depends on the degree of parallelism, the size of the table, and the availability of resources. In general, parallel query can provide significant performance gains for larger tables and high-concurrency workloads.

2. Parallel DML: In this method, the processing of a DML (Data Manipulation Language) statement such as INSERT, UPDATE, or DELETE is divided into multiple smaller tasks that are executed concurrently by multiple CPUs or nodes. Each parallel DML operation has a degree of parallelism, which indicates the number of parallel execution servers that will be used.

For example, consider an INSERT statement to insert a large number of rows into a table:

```
INSERT INTO orders (order_id, customer_id, order_date)
SELECT order_id, customer_id, order_date FROM new_orders;
```

If the number of rows to be inserted is large, the statement can be parallelized to improve the performance:

```
INSERT /*+ append parallel(orders, 4) */ INTO orders (order_id, customer_id,
    order_date)
SELECT order_id, customer_id, order_date FROM new_orders;
```

In this example, we are using parallel DML with a degree of parallelism of 4. This means that the INSERT statement will be divided into 4 smaller tasks and each task will be executed by a separate parallel execution server.

The impact of parallel DML on performance depends on the degree of parallelism, the size of the table, and the availability of resources. In general, parallel DML can provide significant performance gains for larger tables and high-concurrency workloads.

3. Parallel Index Creation: In this method, the creation of an index on a large table is divided into multiple smaller tasks that are executed concurrently by multiple CPUs or nodes. Each parallel index creation operation has a degree of parallelism, which indicates the number of parallel execution servers that will be used.

For example, consider the creation of an index on a large table:

```
CREATE INDEX idx_orders ON orders (order_date);
```

If the table is large, the index creation can be parallelized to improve the performance:

```
CREATE /*+ parallel(orders, 4) */ INDEX idx_orders ON orders (order_date);
```

In this example, we are using parallel index creation with a degree of parallelism of 4. This means that the index creation will be divided into 4 smaller tasks and each task will be executed by a separate parallel execution server.

The impact of parallel index creation on performance depends on the degree of parallelism, the size of the table, and the availability of resources. In general, parallel index creation can provide significant performance gains for larger tables and high-concurrency workloads.

4. Parallel Backup and Recovery: In this method, the backup or recovery of a database is divided into multiple smaller tasks that are executed concurrently by multiple CPUs or nodes. Each parallel backup or recovery operation has a degree of parallelism, which indicates the number of parallel execution servers that will be used.

For example, consider the backup of a large database:

```
RMAN> BACKUP DATABASE PLUS ARCHIVELOG;
```

If the database is large, the backup can be parallelized to improve the performance:

```
RMAN> BACKUP /*+ parallelism(4) */ DATABASE PLUS ARCHIVELOG;
```

In this example, we are using parallel backup with a degree of parallelism of 4. This means that the backup operation will be divided into 4 smaller tasks and each task will be executed by a separate parallel execution server.

The impact of parallel backup and recovery on performance depends on the degree of parallelism, the size of the database, and the availability of resources. In general, parallel backup and recovery can provide significant performance gains for larger databases and high-concurrency workloads.

In conclusion, parallelism can significantly improve the performance of Oracle databases for larger tables and high-concurrency workloads. However, the impact of parallelism on performance depends on several factors such as the degree of parallelism, the size of the table or database, and the availability of resources. It is recommended to perform thorough testing and analysis before implementing parallelism in a production database.

5.3   What are the key features and benefits of Oracle's In-Memory Database Cache, and how does it improve query performance?

Oracle's In-Memory Database Cache, also known as Oracle TimesTen, is a memory-optimized relational database management system that is designed to enhance the performance of real-time applications by storing and managing data in-memory, rather than on disk.

Some of the key features and benefits of Oracle's In-Memory Database Cache are:

1. Faster query performance: By storing data in-memory, Oracle TimesTen can provide much faster query performance compared to disk-based databases. This is because accessing data from memory is much faster than accessing it from disk, which means that queries can be executed much more quickly.

2. High availability: Oracle TimesTen provides high availability and fault tolerance through features such as automatic data replication and failover. This ensures that critical operations are not impacted by database failures, and that data is always available to applications.

3. Scalability: Oracle TimesTen can scale horizontally across multiple servers, allowing applications to scale seamlessly as demand increases. This helps to ensure that application performance remains consistent, even as the volume of data increases.

4. Real-time analytics: With Oracle TimesTen, businesses can perform real-time analytics on large datasets, thereby enabling faster decision-making and improved operational efficiency.

5. Integration with Oracle Database: Oracle TimesTen can be integrated with Oracle Database, allowing businesses to use a combination of in-memory and disk-based storage to optimize performance and reduce costs.

So, how does Oracle TimesTen improve query performance?

Oracle TimesTen improves query performance by storing data in-memory, which reduces the time required to access data from disk. This means that queries can be executed much more quickly, as the data is already in memory and doesn't need to be read from disk.

Additionally, Oracle TimesTen uses optimized algorithms for query processing, which further improves query performance. For example, Oracle TimesTen uses a variety of indexing techniques, such as B-trees and hash indexes, to speed up query execution. It also uses compressed data storage and optimized caching to minimize the amount of data that needs to be read from memory, which helps to further reduce query response times.

In conclusion, Oracle's In-Memory Database Cache, or Oracle TimesTen, is a memory-optimized RDBMS that provides faster query performance, high availability, scalability, real-time analytics, and integration with Oracle Database. By storing data in-memory and using optimized algorithms for query processing, Oracle TimesTen can significantly improve the performance of real-time applications that require fast, efficient access to large datasets.

5.4   Can you explain the Oracle Maximum Availability Architecture (MAA) and its components for ensuring high availability?

Oracle Maximum Availability Architecture (MAA) is a set of best practices and solutions for achieving high availability, performance, and scalability of Oracle databases. It is a comprehensive framework that includes hardware, software, and process components for building and designing highly available systems that meet business-critical service level agreements (SLAs).

The MAA is based on the following four components:

1. System Availability: System availability refers to the ability of the database to consistently provide the required level of service in the face of planned or unplanned downtime events. Oracle achieves high system availability through two methods:

- Redundancy: Redundancy involves having a secondary system or systems that can immediately take over and continue providing service in the event of a failure. Oracle provides several options for redundancy, such as clustering, data guard, and active data guard.

- Fault Tolerance: Fault tolerance refers to the ability of a system to continue functioning in the event of a hardware or software failure, without any data loss or interruption of service. Oracle provides several features that can help achieve fault tolerance, such as automatic storage management (ASM), real application clusters (RAC), and automatic workload management (AWM).

2. Data Protection: Data protection refers to ensuring that data can be retrieved in the event of data loss or corruption. The following are some of the technologies and techniques used in data protection:

- Backup and Recovery: Oracle provides several options for backup and recovery, such as Recovery Manager (RMAN), Oracle Secure Backup, and Oracle Data Guard.

- Disaster Recovery: Disaster recovery involves the ability to recover from a total site failure. Oracle provides several options to implement disaster recovery, such as Oracle Data Guard, Oracle Streams, and Oracle GoldenGate.

- High Availability Storage: Oracle supports high availability storage, which provides advanced features such as redundancy, high-speed access, and rapid recovery from hardware failures.

3. Scalability: Scalability refers to the ability of a system to handle increasing workload demands without compromising performance, reliability, or availability. Oracle provides several features that can help achieve scalability, such as real application clusters (RAC), automatic workload management (AWM), Partitioning and compression.

4. Manageability: Manageability refers to the ability to monitor, diagnose, and resolve issues in a timely manner. Oracle provides several tools and features that can help in manageability, such as Real Application Testing (RAT), Oracle Enterprise Manager (OEM), and Oracle Database 11g Health Check Monitoring.

In summary, Oracle MAA provides a comprehensive set of technologies and solutions for ensuring high availability, performance, scalability, and manageability of Oracle databases. The components of MAA, such as system availability, data protection, scalability, and manageability, work together to provide a holistic approach to building highly available systems that meet business-critical SLAs.

5.5 What are the best practices for managing and optimizing the use of Oracle's Redo Log and Archive Log?

Managing and optimizing the use of Redo Log and Archive Log are crucial for ensuring efficient and reliable Oracle Database performance. In this answer, I will discuss the best practices for managing Redo Log and Archive Log in Oracle Database.

Redo Log:

The Redo Log is a key component of Oracle Database. It stores all changes made to the database, including inserts, deletes, and updates. The Redo Log is responsible for recovering the database in case of a failure or crash. Here are the best practices for managing Redo Log:

1. Sizing Redo Log appropriately: The Redo Log should be sized appropriately to accommodate the rate of change in the database. It is crucial to set the Redo Log size based on the application workload. The size can be increased or decreased as per the need.

2. Multiple Redo Log Groups: It is recommended to have multiple Redo Log groups for high availability and performance. Having multiple groups ensures that logging continues uninterrupted, even if one of the groups fails.

3. Online Redo Log Backup: It is important to take an online backup of the Redo Log to ensure that data is available in the event of a recovery operation. Oracle recommends that you backup the redo log files regularly to protect against data loss.

4. Monitor Redo Log Switches: Monitoring Redo Log Switches is important to ensure optimal performance. High number of Redo Log switches can affect performance negatively. It is important to set the

Redo Log Buffer size properly to avoid too many frequent Redo Log switches.

Archive Log:

The Archive Log is a copy of the Redo Log file that is archived for long-term storage. The Archive Log is a critical component of disaster recovery and is used to roll forward or backward changes if a recovery operation is needed. Here are the best practices for managing Archive Log:

1. Enable Archive Log Mode: Archive Log Mode should be enabled to ensure data recovery in case of a disaster. This mode archives the Redo Log files so that they can be used during a recovery operation.

2. Multiple Archive Destinations: It is recommended to have multiple archive destinations for high availability and disaster recovery. Having multiple destinations ensures that the Archive Log is copied to multiple locations and is available for recovery.

3. Archived Redo Log Backup: It is important to backup the Archived Redo Logs regularly to protect against data loss. In addition, it is important to test the backup regularly to ensure that it can be used in a recovery operation.

4. Monitor Archive Log Disk Space Usage: Monitoring Archive Log Disk Space Usage is important to ensure optimal performance. Archive Log files should be deleted when they are no longer needed. It is important to set up an automatic Archive Log Deletion policy to avoid full disk/file system errors.

In conclusion, managing and optimizing the use of Redo Log and Archive Log in Oracle Database is crucial for ensuring efficient and reliable database performance. By following the best practices outlined above, you can ensure that your database is always available and recoverable in case of a disaster.

5.6 How do you implement Transparent Data Encryption (TDE) in Oracle databases to protect sensitive data at rest?

Transparent Data Encryption (TDE) is a mechanism of encrypting sensitive data stored in database columns, tablespace and backups, where the encryption and decryption of the data is performed transparently, without the user or application being aware of it. The encryption keys are stored in an external wallet, which is encrypted using a master key that is stored outside the database. In this way, TDE provides an additional layer of security to protect sensitive data at rest, in cases where the database or backups are stolen or lost.

To implement TDE in an Oracle database, follow the steps below:

1. Enable the TDE feature in the database by setting the initialization parameter "encryption_enabled" to true. This parameter can be set in the "init.ora" file or using the ALTER SYSTEM command.

Example:

```
ALTER SYSTEM SET encryption_enabled = true;
```

2. Create an Oracle Wallet, which will contain the encryption key used to encrypt and decrypt the data. The wallet must be created outside the database, and its location and password must be specified in the "sqlnet.ora" configuration file.

Example:

Create Wallet:

```
$ORACLE_HOME/bin/mkstore -wrl /u01/app/oracle/wallet -create
```

Open Wallet:

```
$ORACLE_HOME/bin/mkstore -wrl /u01/app/oracle/wallet -createCredential oracle
      database
```

3. Generate a master key, which will be used to encrypt the encryption key stored in the Oracle Wallet. The master key must be created

with a strong password and stored outside the database, to maintain
the security of the encryption keys.

Example:

```
ALTER SYSTEM SET wallet_key_algorithm = 'AES256' scope=spfile;

SHUTDOWN IMMEDIATE;
STARTUP;

CREATE SYSTEM DECRYPT IDENTIFIED BY "password";

ALTER SYSTEM SET ENCRYPTION WALLET OPEN IDENTIFIED BY "password";

ALTER SYSTEM SET ENCRYPTION KEY IDENTIFIED BY "password";
```

4. Encrypt the existing sensitive data using the Oracle Data Pump
Utility or the DBMS_CRYPTO package. The columns, tablespaces
or backups to be encrypted must be specified as part of the command.

Example:

```
-- Encrypt a tablespace
ALTER TABLESPACE users ENCRYPT;

-- Encrypt a column in a table
ALTER TABLE employees MODIFY (salary ENCRYPT);

-- Encrypt a backup
RMAN> CONFIGURE ENCRYPTION FOR DATABASE ON;
RMAN> BACKUP DATABASE PLUS ARCHIVELOG;
```

5. Test the encryption by querying the encrypted data and verifying
that it is not readable in plaintext.

Example:

```
SELECT salary FROM employees;
```

6. Backup and recover the encrypted data and verify that the data
remains encrypted after recovery. The wallet must be backed up separately to ensure the ability to restore or recover the data as needed.

Example:

```
-- Backup the wallet
$ORACLE_HOME/bin/orapki wallet export -wallet /u01/app/oracle/wallet -output
    /u01/app/oracle/backup/wallet -pwd "password"

-- Backup the database
```

```
RMAN> BACKUP DATABASE PLUS ARCHIVELOG;

-- Recover the database
RMAN> RESTORE DATABASE PLUS ARCHIVELOG;
RMAN> RECOVER DATABASE PLUS ARCHIVELOG;
```

5.7 What are the key differences between Oracle's Exadata and traditional database systems in terms of performance and functionality?

Oracle's Exadata is a specialized database appliance that is designed to deliver extreme performance for both Online Transaction Processing (OLTP) and Data Warehousing workloads. In comparison to traditional database systems, Exadata provides significant differences in terms of performance, functionality, and architecture.

Performance Differences: Exadata provides a high-performance architecture that leverages a combination of hardware and software optimizations. The hardware components include Intel Xeon processors, flash memory, and a high-speed InfiniBand network. The software components include Exadata-specific optimizations such as Smart Flash Cache, Smart Scan, and Hybrid Columnar Compression.

Smart Flash Cache is a feature that uses flash memory to cache frequently accessed data blocks. This reduces the need to access data from disk, resulting in faster response times.

Smart Scan is another feature that offloads data filtering and processing from the database server to the Exadata Storage Server. This enables faster retrieval and processing of large data sets.

Hybrid Columnar Compression is a feature that reduces the storage space required for large, historical data sets. By organizing data in a columnar format, compression ratios can be significantly increased, resulting in lower disk space requirements and faster query response times.

Functionality Differences: Exadata provides significant functionality advantages over traditional database systems. Some of the key differences are as follows:

- Integrated Hardware and Software: Exadata provides an all-in-one solution with hardware and software integrated and optimized for maximum performance.

- Automatic Storage Management (ASM): Exadata uses ASM to automatically manage and optimize storage allocation for data files, control files, and log files. ASM simplifies database administration and improves performance.

- Oracle Database Machine: Exadata is a pre-built, pre-configured, and pre-tested turnkey solution that combines hardware, software, and storage. This reduces the deployment time and costs for organizations.

Architecture Differences:
Exadata uses a unique architecture that separates the database and storage servers, and enables parallel processing of queries. This architecture reduces the need for complex storage area network (SAN) configurations and improves performance.

Exadata Storage Server:
The Exadata Storage Server is a specialized server that is optimized for high-performance storage. Each server is equipped with flash memory and high-capacity disks, organized in a high-performance storage grid. The Exadata Storage Server provides a powerful platform for storing and processing large amounts of data.

Database Server:
The database server in Exadata is optimized for parallel processing of queries using a large number of CPU cores and high-speed memory. The database server is connected to the Exadata Storage Server through a high-speed InfiniBand network, enabling fast data transfer between the two servers.

In conclusion, Exadata provides significant performance, functionality, and architecture advantages over traditional database systems. These advantages enable organizations to process large, complex workloads with faster response times, lower storage costs, and simplified administration.

5.8 Can you explain the different types of Oracle partitioning strategies and their impact on query performance?

Oracle partitioning is a powerful feature that can improve the performance and manageability of large database tables. There are several types of partitioning strategies in Oracle, each with its own strengths and weaknesses. In this answer, I will explain the four most common types of partitioning strategies and their impact on query performance.

1. Range partitioning: This strategy divides a table into partitions based on a range of values. For example, you could create a partition for each month of sales data in a table. This can be especially useful for tables that have a date or timestamp column with a high degree of selectivity. Queries that use predicates on the partition key (e.g. WHERE sales_date >= '2021-01-01') can skip over entire partitions, leading to significant performance improvements. Here's an example of how you could create a range-partitioned table:

```
CREATE TABLE sales_data (
  -- Columns go here
)
PARTITION BY RANGE (sales_date) (
  PARTITION p1 VALUES LESS THAN (TO_DATE('2021-02-01', 'YYYY-MM-DD')),
  PARTITION p2 VALUES LESS THAN (TO_DATE('2021-03-01', 'YYYY-MM-DD')),
  PARTITION p3 VALUES LESS THAN (TO_DATE('2021-04-01', 'YYYY-MM-DD'))
);
```

2. List partitioning: This strategy divides a table based on a discrete list of values. For example, you could partition a customer table based on their country of origin. This can be particularly useful for tables that have a low degree of selectivity but must be partitioned for administrative reasons. Queries that use predicates on the partition key can still skip over entire partitions, but there may be less performance improvement compared to range partitioning. Here's an example of how you could create a list-partitioned table:

```
CREATE TABLE customer_data (
  -- Columns go here
)
PARTITION BY LIST (country) (
  PARTITION p1 VALUES ('USA', 'Canada'),
  PARTITION p2 VALUES ('Mexico', 'Brazil'),
  PARTITION p3 VALUES ('UK', 'France', 'Germany')
);
```

3. Hash partitioning: This strategy uses a hashing algorithm to distribute data across partitions based on a chosen column. For example, you could create a hash-partitioned table on a customer_id column. This can be useful for tables that don't have an obvious partition key or for distributing data evenly across partitions. Queries that use predicates on the partition key may not be able to skip over partitions, which can reduce performance compared to range or list partitioning. Here's an example of how you could create a hash-partitioned table:

```
CREATE TABLE customer_data (
  -- Columns go here
)
PARTITION BY HASH (customer_id) PARTITIONS 4;
```

4. Composite partitioning: This strategy combines multiple partitioning strategies into a single table. For example, you could create a table that's range-partitioned by sales_date and then list-partitioned by country. This can be useful for tables that have multiple dimensions that need to be partitioned, but it can also be more complex to manage. The impact on query performance depends on the specific combination of partitioning strategies being used. Here's an example of how you could create a composite-partitioned table:

```
CREATE TABLE sales_data (
  -- Columns go here
)
PARTITION BY RANGE (sales_date)
SUBPARTITION BY LIST (country) (
  PARTITION p1 VALUES LESS THAN (TO_DATE('2021-02-01', 'YYYY-MM-DD'))
  (SUBPARTITION p1usa VALUES ('USA'),
   SUBPARTITION p1canada VALUES ('Canada')),
  PARTITION p2 VALUES LESS THAN (TO_DATE('2021-03-01', 'YYYY-MM-DD'))
  (SUBPARTITION p2mexico VALUES ('Mexico'),
   SUBPARTITION p2brazil VALUES ('Brazil')),
  PARTITION p3 VALUES LESS THAN (TO_DATE('2021-04-01', 'YYYY-MM-DD'))
  (SUBPARTITION p3uk VALUES ('UK'),
   SUBPARTITION p3france VALUES ('France'),
   SUBPARTITION p3germany VALUES ('Germany'))
);
```

Overall, Oracle partitioning can significantly improve query performance for large tables. The specific type of partitioning strategy to use depends on the characteristics of the table and the queries that will be run against it. It's important to choose the right partitioning keys and partitioning schemes for your database to maximize the benefits of partitioning.

5.9 How do you use Oracle's SQL Plan Management (SPM) feature to manage and control execution plans for optimal performance?

Oracle's SQL Plan Management (SPM) feature is designed to manage and control execution plans for optimal performance in Oracle databases. It enables the database to automatically capture and evaluate execution plans for SQL statements, and choose the best plan for execution.

SPM can be used to control and manage execution plans by performing the following tasks:

1. Automatic plan capture: SPM automatically captures execution plans for all SQL statements that are executed as part of the workload.

2. Plan selection: SPM selects the best execution plan for each SQL statement based on the performance of the plans in the SQL plan baseline.

3. Plan evolution: SPM can automatically evolve execution plans over time by comparing new plans to existing ones in the SQL plan baseline, and accepting new plans that are better than the existing ones.

4. Plan verification: SPM can verify the performance of new execution plans before accepting them into the SQL plan baseline.

5. Plan removal: SPM can remove poorly performing execution plans from the SQL plan baseline to ensure that they are not selected for execution in the future.

To use SPM, the following steps are recommended:

1. Enable Automatic Plan Capture: Firstly, you need to enable automatic plan capture by setting the initialization parameter optimizer_capture_sql_plan_baselines to true.

2. Create a SQL Plan Baseline: You then need to create an SQL plan baseline using the DBMS_SPM.CREATE_SQL_PLAN_BASELINE procedure. This baseline specifies which execution plans are acceptable for a particular SQL statement.

3. Load the plan capture information: Once the SQL plan baseline is created, you can load the plan capture information by running the DBMS_SPM.LOAD_PLANS_FROM_CURSOR_CACHE or

DBMS_SPM.LOAD_PLANS_FROM_SQLSET procedure.

4. Evolve plans: You can then introduce new execution plans into the SQL
plan baseline by running the DBMS_SPM.EVOLVE_SQL_PLAN_BASE-
LINE procedure. This procedure compares new plans to existing ones and
accepts the better plan.

5. Perform analysis of SPM performance: You are would need to monitor
the performance of SPM over time to ensure that it is working correctly.
You can do this by querying the V$SQL_PLAN view to see the execution
plans for each SQL statement, and the DBA_SQL_PLAN_BASELINES
view to see the execution plans that are part of the SQL plan baseline.

Below is an example of how to use SPM to manage execution plans:

```
-- Enable automatic plan capture
ALTER SYSTEM SET optimizer_capture_sql_plan_baselines=true;

-- Create an SQL plan baseline for a particular SQL statement
EXEC DBMS_SPM.CREATE_SQL_PLAN_BASELINE(sql_handle => 'INSERT␣INTO␣my_table␣
     VALUES␣(:B1,␣:B2)',
  plan_name => 'my_plan', owner => 'my_schema');

-- Load the plan capture information from the cursor cache for the SQL
     statement
EXEC DBMS_SPM.LOAD_PLANS_FROM_CURSOR_CACHE(sql_text => 'INSERT␣INTO␣my_table␣
     VALUES␣(:B1,␣:B2)');

-- Evolve the SQL plan baseline to introduce new execution plans
EXEC DBMS_SPM.EVOLVE_SQL_PLAN_BASELINE(sql_handle => 'INSERT␣INTO␣my_table␣
     VALUES␣(:B1,␣:B2)',
  plan_name => 'my_plan');

-- Analyze the performance of SPM by querying the V$SQL_PLAN and
     DBA_SQL_PLAN_BASELINES views
SELECT * FROM V$SQL_PLAN WHERE sql_id = 'sql_id';

SELECT * FROM DBA_SQL_PLAN_BASELINES WHERE sql_handle = 'sql_handle';
```

In conclusion, SPM is a powerful feature that can help manage and
control execution plans for optimal performance. With proper setup
and frequent analysis, it can greatly improve the performance of a
database.

5.10   What is the role of Oracle's Automatic Database Diagnostic Monitor (ADDM) in identifying and resolving performance issues?

The Automatic Database Diagnostic Monitor (ADDM) is a built-in feature of Oracle Database that helps to diagnose and resolve database performance issues. The ADDM provides automatic performance analysis of the database showing a detailed report that identifies performance problems, recommends solutions, and even provides specific command-line scripts to implement suggested changes. The ADDM analyzes performance data in the database's Automatic Workload Repository (AWR) to provide diagnostic information about the database. The AWR collects and aggregates performance-related data in the database on an ongoing basis, essentially acting as a time-series database of performance metrics, ensuring accurate tracking of performance problems over time.

When a performance issue arises, the ADDM automatically analyzes the data in AWR, identifying any area of bottlenecks, poor SQL performance or configuration issues that are impacting the performance of the system. The ADDM uses Artificial Intelligence to analyze the workload and the configuration of the database looking for patterns of poor performance, unusual spikes or any situation that can cause problems.

Once the ADDM has identified the performance issues, it presents a detailed report that provides suggestions for resolving the problem. In the report, there is an analysis of the issue, the root cause of the problem, its impact on the database, and remedial actions to be taken.

Here is an example of an ADDM report:

```
Analysis Period: 10:00 - 11:00

Analysis Type: ADDM High Load SQL Analysis

Finding 1: SQL ID 12345678 consumed significant database time
  Impact: High: consumes significant database time (30%)

Recommendation: Tune SQL, add an index or change instance configuration
Script: Run SQL Tuning Advisor on SQL ID, Implement index

Finding 2: Instance configuration has suboptimal settings
```

```
Impact: High

Recommendation: Change instance parameter, SGA size or database block size
Script: Run DBMS_ADVISOR Tuning Task on Instance configuration
```

The database administrator then takes the recommendation and implements the suggested remedies, which may include tuning SQL statements, adding indexes, modifying database configuration, or using additional hardware resources.

In summary, the ADDM is a powerful feature of Oracle Database that provides automated analysis and tuning of database performance. Its strength lies in the ability to analyze the database workload, identify performance bottlenecks, and provide recommendations for their remediation, making it a valuable tool for database administrators in tuning Oracle database performance.

5.11   Can you describe the process of configuring and managing Oracle Real Application Testing (RAT) for simulating production workloads?

Oracle Real Application Testing (RAT) is a tool that is used to simulate a production workload, capture it and then replay it on a test system to ensure that the test system is able to handle the production workload. The process of configuring and managing Oracle Real Application Testing (RAT) involves the following steps:

1. Create a test database: The first step is to create a test database that is similar to the production database. This includes setting up database parameters, creating the necessary tablespaces, and importing any necessary data.

2. Set up the capture environment: The capture environment is the environment where the production workload is captured. This involves installing and configuring the Oracle Database Replay Capture tool on the production system.

3. Capture the production workload: Once the capture environment

is set up, the production workload can be captured. This involves capturing the SQL statements and the workload characteristics, such as the number of users, the concurrency level, and the think time.

4. Transfer the workload to the test environment: Once the production workload is captured, it needs to be transferred to the test environment. This involves copying the workload files to the test system.

5. Set up the replay environment: The replay environment is the environment where the production workload is replayed. This involves installing and configuring the Oracle Database Replay Replay tool on the test system.

6. Replay the workload: Once the replay environment is set up, the production workload can be replayed on the test system. This involves replaying the SQL statements with the same characteristics as the production workload.

7. Analyze the results: Once the replay is complete, the results need to be analyzed. This involves comparing the performance of the test system to the performance of the production system to ensure that the test system can handle the production workload.

Some additional configuration and management tasks related to Oracle Real Application Testing (RAT) include:

- Configuring Database Replay options, such as specifying the capture and replay mode, enabling or disabling SQL tracing, and specifying the capture filter criteria.

- Managing Database Replay, such as starting or stopping Database Replay, viewing the status of Database Replay, and identifying and resolving any issues that may arise during the capture or replay process.

- Monitoring the performance of the test system during the replay to ensure that it does not experience any performance issues. This involves monitoring database metrics, such as CPU usage, memory usage, and disk I/O, as well as application-specific metrics, such as response time and throughput.

Overall, configuring and managing Oracle Real Application Testing (RAT) requires a good understanding of both the production and test environments, as well as an understanding of the tools and options

available within Oracle Real Application Testing (RAT). With proper
setup and management, Oracle Real Application Testing (RAT) can
provide an efficient and effective way to simulate production workloads and identify performance issues before they affect the production system.

5.12   How do you use Oracle's Resource Manager to allocate and manage database resources efficiently?

Oracle's Resource Manager is a powerful tool that enables database
administrators to allocate and control database resources efficiently
based on business priorities. This tool allows the administrator to
define various resource plans and associate each plan to individual
users, groups, or services.

Below are the steps to use Oracle's Resource Manager to allocate and
manage database resources:

1. Create a Resource Plan: A resource plan is used to specify the
allocation of resources between different resource consumer groups.
A resource plan consists of a set of resource consumer groups and
directives for how database resources are to be allocated to these
groups.

For example, the following SQL statement creates a resource plan
named "MY_PLAN" with two consumer groups "OLTP_GROUP"
and "DSS_GROUP":

```
CREATE RESOURCE PLAN my_plan;

CREATE CONSUMER GROUP oltp_group;

CREATE CONSUMER GROUP dss_group;

ALTER RESOURCE PLAN my_plan
    ADD CONSUMER GROUP oltp_group
        EXPLICIT MAPPING CPU_WEIGHT 80;

ALTER RESOURCE PLAN my_plan
    ADD CONSUMER GROUP dss_group
        EXPLICIT MAPPING CPU_WEIGHT 20;
```

In the above example, we have created two consumer groups, OLTP_GROUP and DSS_GROUP, and each group has an explicit mapping of CPU_WEIGHT to represent the proportion of CPU allocated to each group.

2. Create and associate Resource Consumer Groups: A resource consumer group represents a set of users or services that share the same resource allocation. A user or service can be associated with only one consumer group.

For example, the following SQL statement creates a user with ID "USER1" and associates it with the OLTP_GROUP consumer group:

```
CREATE USER user1 IDENTIFIED BY password;

ALTER USER user1 RESOURCE_CONSUMER_GROUP oltp_group;
```

3. Define Resource Directives: Resource directives specify how resources are to be allocated to the resource consumer groups. A resource directive comprises a resource allocation method and a resource allocation limit.

For example, the following SQL statement creates a resource directive to limit CPU usage for the OLTP_GROUP to 50

```
ALTER RESOURCE PLAN my_plan
   MODIFY CONSUMER GROUP oltp_group
      CPU_P1_LIMIT 50;
```

In the above example, the CPU_P1_LIMIT directive limits the CPU usage for OLTP_GROUP to 50

4. Activate Resource Plan: Once the resource plan is configured, it needs to be activated to take effect.

For example, the following SQL statement activates resource plan MY_PLAN:

```
ALTER SYSTEM SET RESOURCE_MANAGER_PLAN = my_plan;
```

This sets the resource manager plan to "MY_PLAN" which means resource allocation for each resource consumer group is as per their defined resource directives.

In conclusion, Oracle's Resource Manager is a very powerful tool to manage and allocate resources based on business priorities. By creating resource plans, consumer groups, and defining directives, administrators can efficiently allocate and manage database resources.

5.13 Can you explain the purpose and functionality of Oracle's Advanced Queuing (AQ) for message processing and queuing?

Oracle's Advanced Queuing (AQ) is an integrated messaging feature in the Oracle database that enables message-based communication between applications. The AQ provides a reliable messaging infrastructure that guarantees the delivery of messages between sender and receiver in a distributed environment, providing a robust solution for message processing and queuing.

The primary purpose of AQ is to facilitate reliable messaging between different components of an application or between different applications. This is achieved by creating a queue where messages can be deposited and retrieved as needed. Messages can be sent to the queue by one component in an application and retrieved by another component in the same or a different application. This facilitates communication and coordination between components or across applications, even when they are running on different servers or different locations.

AQ operates in a publish-subscribe model: publishers create messages and post them to a queue or topic, while subscribers receive the messages from the queue or topic. Unlike traditional messaging systems, AQ provides message persistence and support for transactions, making it suitable for mission-critical applications. The messages are stored in a durable, persistent store and can be retrieved by subscribers even if the server fails or if a network connection is lost.

AQ supports three types of queues: Normal, Exception and Delay queues. Normal queues are the standard queues for storing messages. Messages are stored in the normal queues, and subscribers retrieve messages from the queue as they become available. Exception queues are for handling messages that cannot be processed. If a message fails validation or processing, it is moved to an exception queue, where it

can be processed later. Delay queues allow messages to be held for
a specified amount of time before being delivered to the subscriber.
This is useful for time-sensitive or batch processing applications.

The AQ is built on top of Oracle's database transactions, so it can
provide atomicity, consistency, isolation, and durability (ACID) properties for message transactions. This ensures that message transactions are treated as part of the database transaction and that they
are managed in a consistent and reliable manner.

Here is an example of how to use AQ from inside Oracle:

```
--Create a queue table
EXECUTE DBMS_AQADM.CREATE_QUEUE_TABLE('my_queue_table', 'SYS.
    AQ$_JMS_TEXT_MESSAGE');
--Create a queue
EXECUTE DBMS_AQADM.CREATE_QUEUE('my_queue', 'my_queue_table');
--Enqueue a message
DECLARE
    enqueue_options DBMS_AQ.ENQUEUE_OPTIONS_T;
    message_properties DBMS_AQ.MESSAGE_PROPERTIES_T;
    message_handle RAW(16);
    message_payload VARCHAR2(100) := 'Hello World!';
BEGIN
    DBMS_AQ.ENQUEUE(
        queue_name => 'my_queue',
        enqueue_options => enqueue_options,
        message_properties => message_properties,
        payload => CAST(message_payload AS SYS.AQ$_JMS_TEXT_MESSAGE),
        msgid => message_handle);
END;
/
--Dequeue a message
DECLARE
    dequeue_options DBMS_AQ.DEQUEUE_OPTIONS_T;
    message_properties DBMS_AQ.MESSAGE_PROPERTIES_T;
    message_handle RAW(16);
    message_payload VARCHAR2(100);
BEGIN
    DBMS_AQ.DEQUEUE(
        queue_name => 'my_queue',
        dequeue_options => dequeue_options,
        message_properties => message_properties,
        payload => CAST(message_payload AS SYS.AQ$_JMS_TEXT_MESSAGE),
        msgid => message_handle);
    DBMS_OUTPUT.PUT_LINE('Dequeued message: ' || message_payload);
END;
/
```

5.14 How do you implement and manage partition-wise joins in Oracle databases for improved query performance?

Partition-wise joins can significantly improve query performance for large datasets in Oracle databases. A partition-wise join is a technique that allows Oracle to join two or more large partitioned tables by performing the join operation on smaller, individual partitions rather than the entire table, thereby reducing the data transfer across different nodes and minimizing the workload on individual nodes.

Here are the steps to implement and manage partition-wise joins in Oracle databases:

1. Partition the tables:

Partitioning is a technique that divides larger tables into smaller and more manageable pieces called partitions, improving the data access and query retrieval time. Oracle offers different types of partitioning options such as range, list, hash, and composite partitions, which can be chosen based on the nature and size of the data.

2. Define partition-specific indexes:

Indexes are essential for query performance, and partition-specific indexes can further improve performance by speeding up the search within individual partitions. Create indexes on the partition key columns to speed up the join query.

3. Enable parallel processing:

Parallel processing allows multiple CPU cores to work simultaneously to process the query, which can improve query performance. Oracle offers the option to enable parallel processing on tables, indexes, and even SQL queries.

4. Use partition-wise join syntax:

Partition-wise join syntax instructs Oracle to perform a partition-wise join rather than a traditional join. To use partition-wise join, use the "'/*+ PARALLEL(table_alias [num_slices]) */"' hint before the

SQL query.

Here is an example of partition-wise join syntax:

```
SELECT /*+ PARALLEL (order_part, 4) */ *
FROM orders_part order_part, customer_part customer_part
WHERE order_part.customer_id = customer_part.customer_id;
```

In this example, the query is joining two partitioned tables, orders_part, and customer_part, on their partition key column, customer_id. The partition-wise join is enabled by the parallel hint with four num_slices, indicating that the join operation is divided into four partitions to be processed in parallel.

5. Monitor and manage partition usage:

Monitor the partition usage through monitoring tools such as Enterprise Manager, AWR report. Identify the partitioning key is still the key that provides the most efficient access to data. The partitioning key once created cannot be modified. If the partitioning key becomes less efficient, it is better to create a new table with a new partitioning key and move the data to the new table.

Partition-wise joins can significantly improve query performance in Oracle databases, especially for large tables. Implementing and managing partition-wise join requires careful considerations of partitioning options, indexes, enabling parallel processing, writing partition-wise join queries, and monitoring/ managing partition usage.

5.15 What are the best practices for managing and optimizing Oracle's Temporary Tablespaces?

Temporary Tablespaces are used to store temporary objects such as sorts, joins, temporary tables, and indexes. The best practices for managing and optimizing Oracle's Temporary Tablespaces are:

1. Properly sizing the Temporary Tablespace:

The size of the Temporary Tablespace should be determined based on the maximum required sort size. Oracle recommends that the size of the Temporary Tablespace should be two or three times larger than the largest sort operation performed by the database. This avoids the need for the database to extend the Temporary Tablespace frequently, which can cause performance issues.

2. Multiple Temporary Tablespaces:

Having multiple Temporary Tablespaces can significantly reduce contention for the Temporary Tablespace. Therefore, it's a best practice to create multiple Temporary Tablespaces to spread out the load.

3. Locality considerations:

Oracle recommends creating temporary tablespaces on separate disks from those used for permanent tablespaces. By doing this, it is possible to avoid the situation where temporaries and permanents must share I/O resources.

4. Autoextend:

Set autoextend for the Temporary Tablespace to avoid the need for manual resizing.

5. Monitor the usage:

It's essential to monitor the usage of Temporary Tablespace regularly. This allows the database administrators to take action before any space issues arise. Oracle provides several views to analyze Temporary Tablespace usage, such as the V$TEMPSPACE_USAGE view.

6. Assure proper space management:

Assure proper space management like optimal size of tempfiles, maxsize of tempfile, correct settings for extend policies, etc. This is important because space is a critical source of contention in creating sort areas.

7. Implement Automatic Management of Temporary Tablespace (AMTT):

Temporary tablespace can be created with the "TEMPFILE" clause indicating "AUTOEXTEND ON NEXT 1m MAXSIZE UNLIMITED". This would enable the Oracle database to automatically manage the space allocated to the temporary tablespace.

Here is an example:

```
CREATE TEMPORARY TABLESPACE TEMP01
TEMPFILE '/u01/oracle/data/TEMP01.dbf' SIZE 500M
AUTOEXTEND ON NEXT 50M MAXSIZE UNLIMITED
EXTENT MANAGEMENT LOCAL;
```

The above command creates a Temporary Tablespace called TEMP01 with a size of 500MB. The Temporary Tablespace will auto-extend by 50MB whenever space runs out, up to an unlimited size.

In conclusion, efficiently managing and optimizing Oracle's Temporary Tablespaces is critical for optimal database performance. Properly sizing the Temporary Tablespace based on the maximum required sort size, creating multiple Temporary Tablespaces, monitoring usage regularly, and implementing Automatic Management of Temporary Tablespace (AMTT) are best practices.

5.16   How do you use Oracle's SQL Performance Analyzer (SPA) to evaluate the impact of system changes on SQL performance?

Oracle SQL Performance Analyzer (SPA) is a tool that helps you to evaluate the performance of SQL statements before and after implementing system changes, such as database upgrades, parameter changes or schema modifications. SPA can also be used to compare the performance of the same SQL statement on different systems or with different execution plans, thus helping to identify the optimal execution path.

The main steps to use SPA are:

1. Create a SQL Tuning Set (STS): an object that collects SQL statements to be evaluated via the SQL Performance Analyzer. STS can be created from AWR (Automatic Workload Repository) snapshots, SQL trace files or directly from a SQL statement.

```
-- Creating SQL Tuning Set using SQL Statement
BEGIN
  DBMS_SQLTUNE.CREATE_SQLSET(sqlset_name => 'my_sqlset', description => 'My␣
      Tuning␣Set');

  DBMS_SQLTUNE.LOAD_SQLSET(sqlset_name => 'my_sqlset', populate_cursor => TRUE
      ,
  sql_text => 'SELECT␣/*+␣FULL(t)␣*/␣COUNT(*)␣FROM␣mytable␣t');
END;
/
```

2. Create a SQL Performance Analyzer task: a task that contains
the system changes to be evaluated and the SQL Tuning Set to be
tested. The task can also include execution options such as concurrency, degree of parallelism and optimization level.

```
-- Creating a SQL Performance Analyzer task
BEGIN
  DBMS_SQLPA.CREATE_ANALYSIS_TASK(sqlset_name => 'my_sqlset', task_name => '
      my_task',
  description => 'My␣SPA␣Task', execution_type => DBMS_SQLPA.
      EXECUTION_TYPE_STANDALONE,
  execution_name => 'SYS_AUTO_SQL_TUNING_TASK', execution_params => NULL);
END;
/
```

3. Execute the SQL Performance Analyzer task: this will compare
the performance of the SQL statements in the Tuning Set before and
after the system changes. The results of the analysis are stored in the
SQL Performance Analyzer repository and can be accessed through
the DBA_SQLSET_STATEMENTS view.

```
-- Executing a SQL Performance Analyzer task
BEGIN
  DBMS_SQLPA.EXECUTE_ANALYSIS_TASK(task_name => 'my_task');
END;
/
```

4. Analyze the SQL Performance Analyzer results: the SPA results
will show you the execution statistics for each SQL statement in the
Tuning Set before and after the system changes, including the execution time, CPU time, buffer gets and disk reads.

```
-- Analyzing SQL Performance Analyzer results
SELECT sql_id, sql_text, execution_time_diff, buffer_gets_diff,
    disk_reads_diff
FROM dba_sqlset_statements
WHERE task_name='my_task'
ORDER BY execution_time_diff DESC;
```

By using SQL Performance Analyzer, you can quickly evaluate the
impact of system changes on SQL performance, and identify any re-
gression issues. SPA can also help you to identify the best execution

plan for a given SQL statement, and validate the performance benefits of such plan changes.

5.17 What is the Oracle GoldenGate technology, and how does it facilitate real-time data replication and integration?

Oracle GoldenGate is a data replication and integration software product, offering real-time data movement and transformation between heterogeneous systems, as well as heterogeneous database platforms, including Oracle, SQL Server, SAP HANA, Teradata, MySQL, and others. GoldenGate is used to achieve high availability, disaster recovery, data integration, database migration, and consolidation.

GoldenGate operates using a log-based mechanism that captures changes made in the source database and then delivers those changes to one or more target databases. The changes are propagated using a lightweight and efficient protocol over the network, resulting in minimum impact on the source system's performance. GoldenGate supports bi-directional replication across platforms, enabling customers to take advantage of the unique features offered by each database platform. It can be used for replicating data between databases, data warehouses, or data centers. Additionally, GoldenGate can be used to consolidate data from multiple sources to a single target database.

GoldenGate provides various benefits including:

1) High Availability: GoldenGate provides high availability by maintaining a standby database that is continuously in sync with the primary database. If the primary database goes down, the standby can take over immediately, minimizing downtime.

2) Zero Downtime Upgrades: GoldenGate can facilitate zero downtime upgrades by replicating the production database to a test environment. Upgrades can be tested on the replica, and once verified, the replica can be switched to the production system, resulting in minimal downtime.

3) Real-Time Data Warehousing: GoldenGate facilitates real-time

data warehousing by replicating data from transactional systems to the data warehouse, thus providing real-time reporting and analytics.

4) Heterogeneous Database Replication: GoldenGate enables replication between different database platforms, reducing the need for data migration and ensuring data consistency across platforms.

Overall, GoldenGate helps organizations to adopt a real-time data replication and integration strategy, enabling them to meet SLAs, minimize downtime, enhance decision-making, and improve their bottom line.

5.18   Can you explain the role of Oracle's Active Data Guard in enhancing database availability and disaster recovery?

Oracle's Active Data Guard is a powerful feature that provides various benefits in enhancing the database availability and disaster recovery capabilities of an Oracle database. It allows read-only access to a physical standby database while applying changes from the primary database in real-time. In this answer, I will explain the important features of Active Data Guard and how it can help in enhancing database availability and disaster recovery.

1. Real-Time Data Protection: Oracle's Active Data Guard provides real-time data protection by continuously applying the redo data from the primary database to the standby database. This ensures that the standby database is always in sync with the primary database, and any changes made to the primary database are immediately available on the standby database. This feature helps in minimizing the risk of data loss and provides high availability of the database.

2. Read-Only Access: Active Data Guard allows read-only access to the standby database while it is still receiving redo data from the primary database. This read-only access can be used for various purposes such as reporting, querying, and testing. By offloading these activities to the standby database, the primary database is relieved of

the additional workload, which improves its performance and reduces its downtime.

3. Fast Failover: Active Data Guard provides fast failover capabilities in case of a disaster. When the primary database goes down, the standby database can be quickly promoted to the primary role, and the application can be redirected to the new primary database. This failover process is fast and automatic, reducing the downtime of the application and ensuring high availability of the database.

4. Zero Data Loss: Active Data Guard can provide zero data loss in case of a disaster by using the Oracle Data Guard Broker. The Broker monitors the redo apply progress of the standby database and ensures that the redo data is successfully applied to the standby database before it is marked as synchronized. This ensures that the standby database has all the changes made to the primary database, and there is no data loss in case of a disaster.

5. Online Maintenance: Active Data Guard allows online maintenance activities to be performed on the standby database while it is still receiving redo data from the primary database. This eliminates the need for a separate maintenance window for the standby database and reduces the downtime of the database.

In conclusion, Oracle's Active Data Guard is a powerful feature that provides various benefits in enhancing the database availability and disaster recovery capabilities of an Oracle database. Its real-time data protection, read-only access, fast failover, zero data loss, and online maintenance features make it an essential component for any mission-critical database system.

5.19 How do you manage and optimize the use of Oracle's Shared Pool for efficient memory utilization?

The Shared Pool in Oracle Database is a vital component for optimizing memory usage and efficient performance. It is a shared area of memory used to store frequently executed SQL statements, procedures, packages, and other objects. Therefore, it needs to be managed and optimized to ensure the best use of memory.

Here are some of the ways to manage and optimize the use of Oracle's Shared Pool:

1. Set the Shared Pool Size: Ensure that the size of the Shared Pool is set appropriately to meet the needs of the database. If the Shared Pool is too small, it can lead to contention and cause performance issues while if it is too large, it may lead to wastage of memory. To set the size, one can use the following command:

```
ALTER SYSTEM SET SHARED_POOL_SIZE = <size> [G|M|K];
```

2. Monitor the Shared Pool: Regularly monitor the usage of the Shared Pool to identify any issues or potential problems. Use tools such as Oracle Enterprise Manager or scripts like "sga_info.sql" or "sga_histogram.sql" to monitor the usage of the Shared Pool.

3. Avoid Hard Parsing: Hard parsing is the process of parsing SQL statements for the first time, which can be CPU intensive and increases the load on the Shared Pool. To avoid hard parsing, use bind variables, stored procedures/packages, and cursor sharing. Bind variables allow Oracle to reuse the SQL statement and its execution plan rather than parsing the same statement repeatedly.

4. Enable Automatic Shared Memory Management (ASMM): ASMM is an automatic tuning feature in Oracle that automatically manages shared pool memory along with other memory components like buffer cache, and it sets the size of the components dynamically based on the workload of the database.

5. Use Result Cache: The Result Cache feature caches the results of queries in the Shared Pool, which can help reduce the execution time of similar or repeating queries. This feature is especially useful for queries that return static data or data that changes infrequently.

6. Tune Shared Pool components: The Shared Pool comprises several components like the Library Cache, Data Dictionary Cache, and Miscellaneous Cache. Tuning these components can help optimize memory usage. For example, setting the size of the Library Cache to an appropriate value can avoid contention issues while accessing packages, triggers, and procedures.

In summary, managing and optimizing the use of Oracle's Shared Pool is crucial for efficient memory utilization and optimal database performance. By regularly monitoring the Shared Pool, avoiding hard parsing, enabling ASMM, using the Result Cache feature, and tuning the Shared Pool components, one can achieve the desired performance and optimal resource utilization.

5.20 What are the key features of Oracle Sharding, and how does it enable linear scalability and geographic distribution of data?

Oracle Sharding is a feature of Oracle Database Enterprise Edition that enables linear scalability and geographic distribution of data. Sharding is the process of horizontal partitioning of data across a group of servers or nodes, where each node contains a subset of the total data. Sharding is a commonly used technique in large-scale applications to distribute the load and increase system availability.

The key features of Oracle Sharding are as follows:

1. Shard key: Oracle Sharding uses a shard key to partition the data across nodes. The shard key is a column or set of columns that are used to distribute the data. The definition of the shard key determines how the data is partitioned across nodes.

2. Partitioning methods: Oracle Sharding supports multiple partitioning methods to distribute the data across nodes. The supported partitioning methods are range, list, and hash partitioning.

3. Automatic data routing: Oracle Sharding provides automatic data routing between nodes. Data is routed to the appropriate node based on the shard key. The data routing is transparent to the application, and the application can access the data as if it is stored in a single node.

4. Location transparency: Oracle Sharding provides location transparency to the application. The application is not aware of the phys-

ical location of the data. The application can access the data using a global name, and Oracle Sharding routes the request to the appropriate node.

5. Automatic shard management: Oracle Sharding provides automatic shard management. The system automatically manages the partitioning of data across nodes and rebalances the data when a node is added or removed from the cluster.

6. High availability: Oracle Sharding provides high availability by replicating the data to multiple nodes. In case of a node failure, the system automatically routes the request to another node with a copy of the data.

Oracle Sharding enables linear scalability by distributing the data across nodes. As the data size grows, more nodes can be added to the cluster to handle the increased load. This results in linear scalability, where the performance of the system increases as more nodes are added.

Oracle Sharding also enables geographic distribution of data by allowing the nodes to be located in different physical locations. This enables the application to access the data from the nearest location, reducing the latency and improving the performance.

In conclusion, Oracle Sharding is a powerful feature of Oracle Database Enterprise Edition that enables linear scalability and geographic distribution of data. It provides automatic data routing, location transparency, automatic shard management, high availability, and supports multiple partitioning methods.

Chapter 6

Guru

6.1 How do you design and implement a high-performance, scalable, and fault-tolerant Oracle database architecture for a large-scale enterprise?

Designing and implementing a high-performance, scalable, and fault-tolerant Oracle database architecture for a large-scale enterprise requires careful consideration of several aspects, including hardware configuration, database design, backup and recovery strategies, and clustering.

Here is a broad overview of the steps involved in designing and implementing such an architecture:

1. Define the requirements and goals: The first step in designing any database architecture is to define the requirements and goals of the application. This includes considerations such as the number of users, data size, peak load, response time, and availability requirements.

2. Choose the appropriate hardware: The next step involves choosing the appropriate hardware for the database servers. This includes considerations such as processor speed, memory, storage capacity, net-

work connectivity, and backup capabilities.

3. Optimize database design: After selecting the hardware, the database itself should be designed to optimize performance, scalability, and fault tolerance. This includes factors such as indexing strategies, partitioning, data distribution, and data replication.

4. Implement backup and recovery strategies: It is essential to implement backup and recovery strategies to ensure that critical data is not lost in the event of a system failure or disaster. This includes regular backups, offsite storage of backups, and testing of restore procedures.

5. Implement clustering for high availability: Clustering is a critical component of any high-performance, scalable, and fault-tolerant database architecture. This involves configuring multiple database servers to work together in a cluster, providing load balancing and failover capabilities.

Here are some additional considerations to keep in mind when designing and implementing a high-performance, scalable, and fault-tolerant Oracle database architecture:

- Use solid-state drives (SSDs) for high-performance storage.

- Choose a high-quality networking solution, such as 10-gigabit Ethernet, to ensure fast data transfer speeds.

- Use Oracle Automatic Storage Management (ASM) to manage storage and improve the performance of Oracle databases running on multiple servers.

- Consider implementing virtualization to increase flexibility and scalability while reducing hardware costs.

- Monitor performance metrics regularly to identify and address potential issues before they become actual problems.

Overall, designing and implementing a high-performance, scalable, and fault-tolerant Oracle database architecture for a large-scale enterprise requires careful planning and attention to detail. However, with the right hardware, database design, backup and recovery strategies, and clustering, it is possible to build a robust and reliable system that meets the needs of even the most demanding applications.

6.2   Can you discuss the internals of the Oracle Cost-Based Optimizer (CBO) and how to influence its decision-making process to optimize complex queries?

The Oracle Cost-Based Optimizer (CBO) is a complex and powerful module of the Oracle Database that is responsible for determining the most efficient method of executing a SQL statement. The CBO evaluates all available access paths, transformations, join methods, and optimization techniques before choosing the best execution plan for a given SQL statement.

The CBO uses statistical information to estimate the cost of different execution plans. It will consider factors such as table size, index selectivity, and the number of rows retrieved to determine the cost of accessing data using different methods. The optimizer will also consider the hardware and system configuration, as well as the configuration of the Oracle Database instance itself, to evaluate the cost of different query plans.

One of the key features of the CBO is its ability to choose the best join method for a given query. By selecting the optimal join method, the CBO is able to minimize the amount of data that needs to be accessed and reduce the overall execution time required to process a complex query. In addition, the CBO can take advantage of Oracle Database features such as materialized views, partitioning, and parallel execution to further optimize complex queries.

To influence the decision-making process of the CBO, there are several strategies that can be employed. One approach is to use hints to suggest specific access paths, transformations, join methods, or hints to the optimizer. Hints are comments that can be added to the SQL statement to provide direction to the CBO. For example, the "INDEX" hint can suggest to the CBO that a specific index should be used to access data.

Another approach is to use statistics to provide more accurate information about the data in the database. The CBO relies heavily on statistics to evaluate the cost of different execution plans. By collecting accurate statistics and ensuring that they are up-to-date, the CBO can make more informed decisions about optimization strategies.

A third approach is to use the Oracle Database Tuning Advisor. The Tuning Advisor is a tool that analyzes SQL statements and suggests potential optimization strategies to the database administrator. The Tuning Advisor can recommend changes to the schema design, table indexes, and other optimization techniques to improve query performance.

Overall, optimizing complex queries in the Oracle Database requires a deep understanding of the internals of the CBO and the ability to use advanced features such as hints, statistics, and the Tuning Advisor to influence the decision-making process of the optimizer. By taking a strategic and methodical approach to query optimization, database administrators can significantly improve the performance and reliability of their databases.

6.3   How do you evaluate and choose between different Oracle high availability and disaster recovery solutions, such as Oracle RAC, Data Guard, and GoldenGate, for specific scenarios?

Oracle offers various high availability and disaster recovery solutions, which can be overwhelming to evaluate and choose from for specific scenarios. In general, the choice of solution depends on the specific needs of your business or organization. Below, I will briefly introduce each solution and discuss factors that should be considered when evaluating and choosing between them.

Oracle Real Application Clusters (RAC): Oracle RAC is a clustering solution that provides high availability and scalability for Oracle databases. It enables multiple nodes to access a single, shared database. In other words, it allows the database to run on multiple servers at the same time. RAC is a reliable solution for environments that require continuous availability and scalability. RAC can provide business continuity by ensuring that your application is still available in the event of hardware or network failures.

Oracle Data Guard: Oracle Data Guard is a disaster recovery solution that provides data protection and high availability for Oracle databases. Data Guard replicates the primary database to one or more standby databases, located either on-premises or in the cloud. In the event of a disaster, the standby database can be activated to take over operations from the primary database. Oracle Data Guard can be used to reduce the risk of data loss or to ensure that database operations are not interrupted in the event of a disaster.

Oracle GoldenGate: Oracle GoldenGate is a real-time data replication and integration solution that allows you to capture, route, and deliver transactional data across heterogeneous systems. GoldenGate can be used to implement high availability and disaster recovery solutions by replicating data in real-time to a standby database, located either on-premises or in the cloud. In the event of a disaster, the standby database can be activated as a primary database. GoldenGate can be used to minimize downtime and data loss during planned and unplanned outages.

When evaluating and choosing between these solutions, the following factors should be considered:

- Recovery Time Objective (RTO): This is the maximum acceptable amount of time that your system can be down in the event of an outage. The lower the RTO, the more expensive the solution may be. For example, if your RTO is short, Oracle RAC may be the better solution as it provides immediate failover, whereas Data Guard requires activation of the standby database.

- Recovery Point Objective (RPO): This is the maximum acceptable amount of data loss in the event of an outage. The lower the RPO, the more expensive the solution may be. For example, if your RPO is short, Oracle GoldenGate may be the better solution as it provides real-time data replication and minimal data loss.

- Budget: Different solutions have different costs. Oracle RAC will generally be the most expensive, followed by Data Guard and GoldenGate. GoldenGate can be more expensive than Data Guard because of its additional features such as real-time data replication and integration.

- Infrastructure: The choice of solution may depend on the infrastructure requirements of your organization. For example, if you have limited hardware resources, Oracle RAC may not be feasible as it requires a shared storage solution.

In summary, each disaster recovery solution provided by Oracle offers its unique features and benefits. Combining these solutions together can provide even better protection against disasters. A thorough evaluation of recovery objectives, budget, and infrastructure requirements can help in choosing the most appropriate solution(s) for your business.

6.4   What are the best practices for implementing Hybrid Columnar Compression (HCC) in Oracle databases, and how does it impact storage efficiency and query performance?

Hybrid Columnar Compression (HCC) is an advanced storage compression technology introduced in Oracle Database 11g. HCC is designed to reduce storage requirements and improve query performance for large-scale data warehouses and archival systems. HCC achieves this efficiency by storing data in columns instead of rows and compressing similar data values together.

Here are some best practices for implementing HCC in Oracle databases:

1. Choose the Right HCC Format: Oracle offers three compressions algorithms: Query Low (QL), Query High (QH), and Archive High (AH). QL compression is best suited for read-mostly systems, QH is well-suited for OLTP systems with high write activity, and AH is ideal for archival data where quick retrieval is not a priority.

2. Define Appropriate Data Segmentation: It is essential to segment data based on access frequency to maximize storage efficiency. Frequently accessed data should not be compressed due to the overhead of decompression during query processing. Segmentation is also necessary to set compression parameters such as block size and column order.

3. Combine HCC with Partitioning: HCC is especially useful when combined with partitioning. The partitioning of data can be based on any criterion, such as time, region, or department, resulting in more

efficient compression.

4. Monitor Compression Ratios: As HCC compression is based on the similarities between data values, it is essential to monitor compression ratios. A low compression ratio implies that there is little redundancy in the data, and HCC may not be optimal for that dataset.

5. Utilize HCC with Exadata: HCC is particularly efficient when used with Exadata, Oracle's specialized hardware designed to work with its database software. This combination can reduce storage requirements and query processing times.

The impact of HCC on storage efficiency and query performance is significant. HCC can reduce storage requirements by 10x to 50x and improve query performance by 3x to 4x. In some cases, depending on the data and workload, customers have achieved up to 70

In conclusion, to achieve the best results with HCC, it is essential to choose the right compression format, segment data effectively, combine it with partitioning, monitor compression ratios, and use it with specialized hardware like Exadata. HCC can offer incredible storage efficiency and query performance gains for large-scale data warehouses and archival systems.

6.5 Can you describe the advanced features of Oracle's Partitioning and Subpartitioning strategies for managing large-scale, distributed data sets?

Oracle Database Partitioning is a powerful feature that enables us to divide large tables and indexes into smaller and more manageable pieces, known as partitions. These partitions permit tables and indexes to be segmented in a very granular way, thus allowing more efficient management and maintenance of large-scale, distributed data sets.

There are a few advanced features of Oracle's partitioning and subpartitioning strategies, which are discussed below:

1. Range partitioning: In range partitioning, data is divided based on a range of values in a particular column. For example, a table can be partitioned by date, and each partition contains data for a specific range of dates.

2. List partitioning: List partitioning divides data based on a specific list of values in a particular column. For example, a table can be partitioned by region, with each partition containing data for a specific region.

3. Hash partitioning: Hash partitioning divides data into partitions based on a hashing algorithm. The algorithm distributes data evenly across all partitions, ensuring that the load is balanced across all the partitions.

4. Composite partitioning: Composite partitioning is a combination of one or more partitioning methods. For example, we can partition data by range, and then partition each range further by hash or list.

5. Subpartitioning: Subpartitioning divides partitions into smaller pieces, thus enabling even more granular management of data. For example, a table can be partitioned by region and then subpartitioned by month.

6. Interval partitioning: Interval partitioning automatically creates new partitions based on a specified time interval. For example, a table can be partitioned by date, and Oracle can automatically create new partitions for each month, based on the defined interval.

7. Virtual column partitioning: Virtual column partitioning allows partitioning of a table based on a virtual column. A virtual column is a column that is not stored physically in the table but is automatically generated based on the values of other columns in the table.

In summary, Oracle's partitioning and subpartitioning strategies offer several advanced features that allow for efficient management of large-scale, distributed data sets. These strategies enable tables and indexes to be segmented in a granular way, enabling more efficient maintenance and management of data.

6.6 How do you design and implement advanced security measures in Oracle databases, including Database Vault, Transparent Data Encryption, and Data Redaction?

Designing and implementing advanced security measures in Oracle databases is an essential part of protecting sensitive information from unauthorized access. In this answer, we'll discuss three popular security measures - Database Vault, Transparent Data Encryption, and Data Redaction - and provide a high-level overview of their implementation.

Database Vault:

Database Vault is a built-in feature of Oracle Database that provides a comprehensive set of advanced security controls to protect the database from privileged user access. Database Vault introduces the concept of realms to enforce security policies that restrict access to sensitive data based on specific criteria such as roles, IP address, time of day, etc. Additionally, it allows organizations to restrict administrative privileges, so the administrative actions must be based on authorization rules which prevent specific operations from occurring in a non-authorized time. The enforcement of the security policies is performed through the database firewall, which is a software component that works in conjunction with other security features to restrict access to sensitive data.

Implementing Database Vault involves a few steps:

1. Installation: The first step is to install the Database Vault option on top of an existing Oracle Database.

2. Configuration: Once installed, the Database Vault configuration process can be initiated using the DVRCTLP utility. The configuration of the Database Vault requires creating the components of the feature such as realms, command rules, and factor rules.

3. Enabling Database Vault policies: After creating the components, Database Vault policies must be enabled to restrict the access to

sensitive data based on specific attributes.

Transparent Data Encryption:

Transparent Data Encryption (TDE) provides an additional layer of protection to Oracle Database by encrypting sensitive data on disk. TDE is a part of Oracle Advanced Security option which encrypts the data in the database's tablespaces, data files, and backups, to avoid data theft and unauthorized data access. The encryption algorithm used by TDE is AES-256, which is a symmetric-key encryption algorithm.

Implementing TDE involves a few steps:

1. Configuring the wallet: The first step is to configure the wallet that stores the encryption keys. The wallet must be created and stored in a secure location, and the wallet password must be known to authorized users who require access to the encrypted data.

2. Creating the TDE tablespace: Once the wallet is configured, a TDE-enabled tablespace can be created, and the underlying data files will be encrypted automatically.

3. Enabling TDE for existing tablespaces: Organisations that have existing non-TDE tablespaces can enable TDE via online tablespace encryption or offline tablespace encryption.

Data Redaction:

Data Redaction is another built-in feature of Oracle Database that offers data masking services for data exposure to non-authorized users. Data Redaction works by replacing sensitive data with fictional but realistic data. The data masking functions can be conditioned to a specific time, user, or role, making it flexible.

Implementing Data Redaction involves three steps:

1. The first step is to create a policy that identifies the sensitive data in the database.

2. The sensitivity types are anonymized by using a redaction function such as full redaction, partial redaction, or regular expression redaction, etc.

3. Finally, the policy must be enabled to apply the data redaction modification to the table attributes.

In conclusion, Oracle database provides an array of built-in security features include Database Vault, TDE, Data Redaction, etc. while following implementation steps to safeguard sensitive information of an organization from unauthorized access. Furthermore, it's recommended to consider implementing robust and unique access controls, identification of who has access to sensitive data, and adherence to industry-specific regulations in the data security strategy.

6.7 What are the key performance considerations when migrating an Oracle database to Oracle Cloud Infrastructure (OCI), and how do you optimize the migration process?

Migrating an Oracle database to Oracle Cloud Infrastructure (OCI) requires careful planning to ensure optimal performance. Some of the key performance considerations when migrating an Oracle database to OCI are:

1. Network Bandwidth: The network connectivity between the on-premises database and the OCI environment can significantly impact performance during migration. It is recommended to use a high-speed, reliable network connection with sufficient bandwidth to minimize downtime and ensure quick migration.

2. Storage Performance: The performance of storage used by the Oracle database is critical for optimal database performance. OCI offers two types of storage options through which a database can be hosted, Block volume storage and File storage. It is important to select the correct storage type according to the workloads.

3. Instance Size: It's essential to select an appropriate compute instance for optimal performance. Selecting a properly sized instance will depend on the workload running on the Oracle database to be migrated. OCI provides a wide range of instance sizes to choose from.

4. Database Size: Larger databases may require additional resources during the migration process. It is recommended to perform pre-migration sizing analysis to ensure that the target OCI database can support the migrated data.

5. Database Compatibility: Ensure the database version is compatible with the targeted OCI environment. OCI provides guidance on compatibility for various databases.

6. Security: Ensure that the security posture of the environment is maintained. OCI provides a robust security infrastructure and guidance to ensure that the security posture of the database is maintained during and after migration.

To optimize the migration process, the following best practices can be followed:

1. Select an appropriate migration method: OCI provides multiple migration methods to use, including Data Transport and Database Migration services, amongst others. Choose the method that best suits the data/migration volume and the available downtime window.

2. Optimize Database Performance: Optimize the performance of the on-premises database during the migration process to minimize the time required to complete the migration.

3. Monitor and adjust resources: During the migration process, monitor the resources being used by the database in OCI and adjust them as required.

4. Review and tune parameters: After the migration is completed, review and tune the database parameters, including block size, buffer cache, and PGA for optimal performance.

5. Perform a comprehensive test: Test the migrated database thoroughly to ensure that it is fully functional and performing as expected.

By following these performance considerations and best practices, organizations can optimize the migration process and ensure optimal performance of their Oracle database on OCI.

6.8 Can you discuss the internals of the Oracle In-Memory Database option and its impact on query performance, especially for analytic and reporting workloads?

Oracle In-Memory Database Option is a feature that enables users to store database tables entirely in memory, providing faster access to the data. The feature was first introduced in Oracle Database 12c and is intended to enhance the performance of analytic and reporting workloads by reducing the time taken to access and manipulate large amounts of data.

When a table is loaded into memory, it is stored in a special columnar format that differs from the traditional row-based format used in disk-based storage. In the columnar format, data for each column is stored together, allowing for faster data access and manipulation. Additionally, the data is compressed in memory, which allows for more data to be loaded into memory and reduces the amount of I/O required to access the data.

Query performance is greatly improved when using the Oracle In-Memory Database Option, especially for analytic and reporting workloads. This is due to the nature of analytic and reporting queries, which typically involve analyzing large amounts of data. By storing the data in memory, the time taken to access and manipulate the data is significantly reduced, leading to faster query performance.

The following query demonstrates how the Oracle In-Memory Database option can be used to improve query performance:

```
SELECT product_category, SUM(sales_amount)
FROM sales_table
WHERE sales_date BETWEEN TO_DATE('01-JAN-2020', 'DD-MON-YYYY')
AND TO_DATE('31-DEC-2020', 'DD-MON-YYYY')
GROUP BY product_category;
```

In this example, the query is used to retrieve the total sales amounts by product category for the year 2020. If the sales_table is loaded into memory using the Oracle In-Memory Database Option, the query will typically run much faster than when accessing the data from disk-based storage.

One thing to note is that the Oracle In-Memory Database Option requires additional memory resources to load the tables into memory, so it's important to ensure that there is enough memory available to support the feature. Additionally, the feature requires a license to use, so it's important to factor in the cost when deciding whether to use the option.

In conclusion, the Oracle In-Memory Database Option is a powerful feature that can greatly improve query performance, especially for analytic and reporting workloads. The feature achieves this by storing data in a columnar format in memory, which allows for faster data access and manipulation. However, the feature requires additional memory resources and a license to use, so it's important to carefully consider these factors when deciding whether to enable the feature for a given database.

6.9   How do you use Oracle's SQL Tuning Advisor and SQL Access Advisor to optimize complex SQL statements and improve overall database performance?

Oracle has several tools to tune SQL statements and improve overall database performance. SQL Tuning Advisor and SQL Access Advisor are two such tools offered by Oracle. These tools use different techniques to diagnose and optimize SQL statements. The SQL Tuning Advisor is a tool that identifies SQL statements that are consuming excessive database resources, such as high CPU, long execution time, excessive I/O or contention. The advisor then recommends changes to the SQL statement or underlying database structure to improve performance. SQL Access Advisor is a tool that recommends indexes and partitioning strategies for tables accessed by SQL statements. In the following sections, we discuss these tools in more detail and provide examples of how to use them.

SQL Tuning Advisor:

The SQL Tuning Advisor is an automated tool that assists in the tuning of SQL statements by identifying performance problems and providing recommendations on how to tune the SQL statement. It analyzes the SQL statement and builds a description of the statement, including all the objects it references, the predicates and joins, and the execution plan. The advisor then uses this information to recommend changes to the SQL statement, such as adding or removing indexes, modifying the SQL statement, or tuning the database structure.

To use the SQL Tuning Advisor, the user submits a SQL statement for analysis, and the tool generates a report containing recommendations for improving the statement's performance. The advisor uses several methods to tune the SQL statement, including the following:

1. Cost-based analysis:

The cost-based analysis is used to optimize the SQL statement by choosing the most efficient execution plan. The advisor evaluates the execution plans generated by the optimizer, identifies the most expensive operations, and suggests alternative plans to improve performance.

2. Access path analysis:

The advisor analyzes the access paths used by the optimizer to fetch data from the tables. It identifies the access paths that are inefficient and makes recommendations to choose the most efficient access paths.

3. Behavior analysis:

The advisor analyzes the behavior of the SQL statement, including the number of rows returned, the number of executions, the data types used, and the SQL features used. It then determines whether the SQL statement is behaving correctly and suggests changes to improve performance.

Here is an example of how to use the SQL Tuning Advisor:

```
-- Create a SQL Tuning Task for a specific SQL statement
DECLARE
    l_sql_tune_task_id VARCHAR2(100);
BEGIN
    l_sql_tune_task_id :=
        DBMS_SQLTUNE.CREATE_TUNING_TASK (
            sql_text => 'SELECT d.department_name, l.city
                                    FROM departments d, locations l
```

```
␣␣␣␣␣␣␣␣␣␣␣␣␣␣␣␣␣␣␣␣␣␣␣␣␣WHERE␣d.location_id␣=␣l.location_id
␣␣␣␣␣␣␣␣␣␣␣␣␣␣␣␣␣␣␣␣␣␣␣␣␣AND␣d.department_name␣LIKE␣''%SALES%''',
        bind_list => '',
        user_name => 'SCOTT',
        scope    => DBMS_SQLTUNE.SCOPE_COMPUTE_AND_ADVICE,
        time_limit=> 1800,
        task_name =>'tune_sales_query'
        );

  DBMS_SQLTUNE.EXECUTE_TUNING_TASK(task_name => 'tune_sales_query');
END;
/

-- Display the results of the SQL Tuning Advisor
SELECT DBMS_SQLTUNE.REPORT_TUNING_TASK('tune_sales_query') AS recommendations
FROM dual;
```

SQL Access Advisor:

The SQL Access Advisor is a tool that recommends indexes and partitioning strategies for tables accessed by SQL statements. It analyzes the SQL workload and the database schema to determine the tables and indexes that require tuning. The advisor provides recommendations on index creation, index modification or removal, partitioning, and subpartitioning.

To use the SQL Access Advisor, the user submits a SQL workload to the tool, and the tool generates a recommendation report for index creation or modification. The SQL workload contains SQL statements and their corresponding execution statistics, including the number of executions, the number of rows returned, and the execution time. The advisor uses this information to recommend the appropriate indexes.

Here is an example of how to use the SQL Access Advisor:

```
-- Create a task to analyze a SQL workload
DECLARE
    task_name VARCHAR2(30);
BEGIN

    task_name := dbms_advisor.create_task (
                advisor_name => 'SQLAccessAdvisor',
                task_name    => 'tune_sales_workload',
                description => 'Recommend␣indexes␣for␣the␣sales␣workload');

    dbms_advisor.create_object (
        task_name   => task_name,
        object_type => 'SQL',
        object_name => 'SELECT␣d.department_name,␣l.city
␣␣␣␣␣␣␣␣␣␣␣␣␣␣␣␣␣␣␣␣␣␣␣␣␣␣␣␣␣FROM␣departments␣d,␣locations␣l
␣␣␣␣␣␣␣␣␣␣␣␣␣␣␣␣␣␣␣␣␣␣␣␣␣␣␣␣␣WHERE␣d.location_id␣=␣l.location_id
␣␣␣␣␣␣␣␣␣␣␣␣␣␣␣␣␣␣␣␣␣␣␣␣␣␣␣␣␣AND␣d.department_name␣LIKE␣''%SALES%''',
        attr1       => DBMS_ADVISOR.SQL_WORKLOAD,
        attr2       => 'SALES_WORKLOAD',
        attr3       => NULL);

    dbms_advisor.execute_task(task_name);
```

```
END;
/

-- View the recommendations
SELECT dbms_advisor.get_task_report('tune_sales_workload') AS recommendations
FROM dual;
```

In summary, SQL Tuning Advisor and SQL Access Advisor are two powerful tools in Oracle that provide recommendations for SQL statement tuning and index creation. These tools can significantly improve the performance of complex SQL statements and databases.

6.10   Can you explain the advanced features of Oracle's Exadata platform, such as Smart Scan, Smart Flash Cache, and Storage Indexes, and their impact on database performance?

Oracle's Exadata platform is designed to deliver high performance for data warehousing and OLTP workloads by integrating hardware and software components in a tightly coupled manner. Some of the advanced features of Exadata that contribute significantly to its performance are Smart Scan, Smart Flash Cache, and Storage Indexes.

Smart Scan is a feature of Exadata storage servers that offloads some filtering and processing of data from the database server to the storage server. When a SQL query is executed, the Exadata storage server scans only the relevant rows and columns of data and sends back only the necessary data that matches the query predicate. This reduces the amount of data that needs to be transmitted across the network, resulting in faster query response times. Smart Scan can provide significant performance improvements for large table scans, as well as queries that involve joins, sorts, and aggregations.

Smart Flash Cache is a feature of Exadata storage servers that uses flash-based solid-state drives (SSDs) to cache frequently accessed data. The flash cache is automatically managed by Exadata and can be used to supplement the main memory (DRAM) of the database server. The flash cache can provide significant performance improvements for random I/O workloads, such as OLTP transactions, by reducing the number of disk accesses required to retrieve data. Since flash memory is faster than traditional magnetic disks, data can be retrieved from the cache much faster than from disk, leading to shorter response times for database queries.

Storage Indexes are another feature of Exadata storage servers that improve query performance by reducing the amount of data that needs to be scanned. Storage Indexes work by keeping track of the minimum and maximum values of certain columns in each storage server. When a SQL query is executed that includes a predicate on the same columns, Exadata can use the stored index information to skip over any storage blocks that do not contain the desired data. This can reduce the amount of disk I/O required to retrieve the necessary data, resulting in faster query execution times.

The impact of these advanced Exadata features on database performance can be significant. For example, Smart Scan can reduce query response times by up to 10x or more for large table scans. Smart Flash Cache can reduce the amount of disk access required for OLTP workloads by up to 90

In conclusion, the advanced features of Oracle's Exadata platform such as Smart Scan, Smart Flash Cache, and Storage Indexes offer significant benefits for data warehousing and OLTP workloads by reducing disk I/O, network traffic, and query execution times. These features are automatically managed by Exadata and do not require any changes to the database schema or applications.

6.11 How do you design and manage an Oracle Multitenant environment for efficient resource utilization, security, and scalability in a large organization?

Designing and managing an Oracle Multitenant environment for efficient resource utilization, security, and scalability in a large organization requires careful planning and implementation. In this answer,

I will provide some best practices and guidelines for designing and managing such an environment.

1. Logical and Physical Design

The logical design of the multitenant environment must consider the organizational hierarchy, the user access controls, and the required levels of separation between tenants. The physical design should ensure that resources are optimized and the hardware is scalable. Considerations such as the number of PDBs on a given server, the number of CPUs and memory allocated to each PDB, and the storage capacity of the server are key to ensuring the environment is scalable, manageability and capacity planning.

2. Resource Utilization

A key advantage of Oracle Multitenant is the efficient use of system resources. To ensure efficient resource utilization, ensure that your databases are properly consolidated and architected for resource sharing where possible. For example, you can share common users (CDB users) between multiple PDBs, rather than creating new copies of these users for each PDB. In order to avoid overloading the system, make sure that the maximum number of concurrent sessions are properly planned and implemented, using the MAX_CONNECTIONS attribute for each PDB.

3. Security and Access Control

In a multitenant environment, security is of the utmost importance. The security infrastructure must be designed to ensure that tenants have secure, isolated environments with separate authentication and authorization. A good practice is to use the CDB users to manage global roles and privileges, avoiding having multiple instances of the same user with different privileges.

4. Backup and Recovery

To ensure recoverability of each PDB in case of unexpected failure, each PDB should be backed up regularly, following a well-defined backup strategy. Ensure that backup/recovery procedures and scripts are properly tested and ensure data validation.

5. Performance Monitoring and Tuning

Effective tuning and monitoring of the environment requires a comprehensive set of metrics and monitoring tools. Oracle offers several tools like The Oracle Enterprise Manager (OEM), which helps detect

and fix performance issues at the PDB level. This tool also offers the
ability to visualize the SQL execution plans for PDB queries.

6. Maintenance and Upgrades
Patching/maintenance for a multitenant environment should be done
with caution as it can affect multiple PDBs at the same time. A
good practice is to test patches/maintenance on non-production PDB
copies first, in order to avoid any unexpected issues. Also, Oracle
offers the ability to isolate and patch a single PDB while the others
remain operational.

In conclusion, to effectively design and manage an Oracle Multitenant
environment for efficient resource utilization, security, and scalability
in a large organization, careful planning and attention need to be
taken in logical and physical design, resource utilization, security,
backup, performance monitoring and tuning, and upgrades/mainte-
nance.

6.12   What are the best practices for im-
plementing and optimizing Oracle's
Automatic Storage Management (ASM)
in large-scale, mission-critical environments?

Oracle's Automatic Storage Management (ASM) provides a simplified and efficient approach to managing storage for Oracle databases.
In large-scale, mission-critical environments, ASM can help improve
performance and availability, but effective implementation and optimization are critical for achieving these benefits.

Here are some best practices for implementing and optimizing ASM
in large-scale, mission-critical environments:

1. Plan carefully

Before implementing ASM, it's important to plan carefully. This includes assessing your storage needs, selecting appropriate hardware
and storage configurations, and determining the best deployment ar-

chitecture.

2. Use redundancy and mirroring

Redundancy and mirroring are essential for ensuring high availability and data protection. ASM provides various mirroring options, including two-way, three-way, and normal/ high redundancy mirroring. Using mirroring judiciously can help ensure data availability despite disk failures.

3. Optimize performance

ASM provides various performance optimizations, including Automatic Data Placement, which ensures that data is placed on the most optimal disk. Use ASM's performance tuning features to ensure optimal performance. For example, adjusting the ASM_PREFERRED_READ_FAILURE_GROUPS parameter can help optimize read performance.

4. Monitor performance regularly

Regular monitoring can help identify performance issues and prevent downtime. Use Oracle Enterprise Manager or ASM's native tools to monitor ASM performance regularly. Check alerts, errors, and performance metrics and make necessary changes to optimize performance.

5. Tune ASM memory parameters

ASM uses memory for caching metadata and data. Proper memory allocation and management can help optimize ASM performance. Adjust the ASM memory parameters such as ASM_DISKGROUPS and ASM_POWER_LIMIT according to the available memory and workload requirements.

6. Use ASM Fast Mirror Resync (FMR)

FMR feature helps to reduce the resync time of mirror disks after a failure. This feature keeps track of the changes of the redundant disk and replays the change in the new disk, instead of copying the entire data. Use FMR to optimize the recovery time of failed disks.

7. Keep ASM software and disk firmware up-to-date

Ensure that ASM software and disk firmware are up-to-date to avoid known bugs or compatibility issues. Oracle frequently releases patches, upgrades, and firmware updates necessary to optimize performance and avoid data corruption.

8. Plan for growth

Ensure that ASM storage is scalable enough to accommodate future growth. Plan expansion and have adequate disk space readily available. Plan for growth to avoid the need for expensive and time-consuming hardware replacement.

In summary, ASM can help improve performance and availability in large-scale, mission-critical environments. Effective implementation and optimization are essential to achieving these benefits. Careful planning, performance tuning and monitoring, periodic updates, and readiness for growth are essential to making ASM work effectively in mission-critical environments.

6.13 Can you discuss advanced Oracle RMAN features, such as Block Change Tracking, TSPITR, and Incrementally Updated Backups, and their impact on backup and recovery performance?

1. Block Change Tracking: Oracle RMAN's Block Change Tracking (BCT) feature helps speed up incremental backups by tracking blocks that have changed since the last backup. This makes it possible to skip scanning blocks that haven't changed, reducing the time required to complete the backup. When enabled, the database writes a file to disk that contains information about the changed blocks, which RMAN uses during the incremental backup process.

Enabling BCT is straightforward - simply set the parameter 'DB_CREATE_FILE_DEST' to a directory where the tracking file can be written. Then, set the parameter 'CHANGE_TRACKING' to 'ON' for each datafile that you want to track changes for. For example:

```
ALTER DATABASE ENABLE BLOCK CHANGE TRACKING USING FILE '<
    path_to_tracking_file>';
ALTER DATABASE DATAFILE '<datafile>' ENABLE BLOCK CHANGE TRACKING;
```

Enabling BCT can improve backup performance significantly, especially for large databases with high rates of change. However, it does
require some extra disk space to store the tracking file, and it may
impact overall database performance since it adds some overhead to
the block modification process.

2. Tablespace Point-in-Time Recovery (TSPITR): Oracle RMAN's
Tablespace Point-in-Time Recovery (TSPITR) feature allows you to
recover one or more tablespaces to a point in time before a problem
occurred. This can be useful if you have a damaged tablespace or if
you accidentally dropped a table or schema.

To perform a TSPITR, you need a backup of the affected tablespaces,
as well as archived redo logs that cover the desired recovery time
period. You'll also need to create a recovery catalog, if you haven't
already done so.

The basic steps to perform a TSPITR are:

- Use RMAN to restore the backup of the affected tablespaces to a separate
location.

- Recover the restored database to the desired point in time using the
archived redo logs.

- Export the recovered tables or tablespaces using Oracle Data Pump or
other export tool.

- Import the exported data into the target database.

TSPITR can be a powerful tool for recovering from certain types of
data loss scenarios. However, it does require some extra steps and
can be time-consuming, particularly if you have a large database or
if you need to recover multiple tablespaces.

3. Incrementally Updated Backups: Oracle RMAN's Incrementally
Updated Backups feature allows you to create an incremental backup
that includes only the changed blocks since the last backup, then
merge that backup into a full backup. This can help reduce backup
windows and storage requirements, as well as provide faster recovery
times.

To perform an Incrementally Updated Backup, you'll need to have a
Level 0 backup of the database, as well as one or more Level 1 backups that were created using the 'BACKUP INCREMENTAL LEVEL
1 CUMULATIVE' command. The basic steps to create an Incrementally Updated Backup are:

- Use RMAN to create a new Level 1 backup using the 'BACKUP IN-
CREMENTAL LEVEL 1 CUMULATIVE' command.

- Run the 'BACKUP INCREMENTAL LEVEL 0 MERGE' command to
merge the Level 1 backup into the existing Level 0 backup.

Incrementally Updated Backups can be a powerful tool for reducing
backup windows and storage requirements, as well as for providing
faster recovery times. However, they do require some extra overhead
to create and maintain the incremental backups, and they may require
more disk space than traditional full backups if you have a high rate
of change in your database.

Overall, these advanced Oracle RMAN features can be very useful for
improving backup and recovery performance, as well as for recovering
from certain types of data loss scenarios. By understanding their
strengths and weaknesses, you can determine which features are best
suited to your specific needs and deploy them accordingly.

6.14   How do you use Oracle's Advanced Compression and Deduplication features to optimize storage utilization and performance in large-scale databases?

Oracle's Advanced Compression and Deduplication features are designed to help organizations optimize storage utilization and performance in large-scale databases.

Advanced Compression is a feature that allows for the compression
of data and indexes within the database. This reduces the amount of
storage required and can improve the performance of queries that access the compressed data. There are several compression algorithms
available, including basic compression, which is relatively light on

CPU usage, and high compression, which requires more CPU resources but offers greater storage savings.

To enable Advanced Compression, you can use the COMPRESS attribute when defining a table or index. For example, to compress a
table named MY_TABLE, you can use the following SQL statement:

```
ALTER TABLE MY_TABLE COMPRESS FOR OLTP;
```

This will enable compression for the table using the OLTP compression algorithm, which is optimized for transactional workloads.

In addition to table and index compression, Oracle also offers compression for backup and recovery operations. This can allow for faster
backup and restore times, as well as reduced storage requirements for
backup files.

Deduplication, on the other hand, is a feature that allows for the
removal of redundant data within the database. This can help to further optimize storage utilization and reduce backup times. Oracle's
deduplication feature is integrated with the backup and recovery functionality, and can be enabled using the RMAN (Recovery Manager)
command-line interface.

To enable deduplication for a backup, you can use the following command:

```
CONFIGURE CHANNEL DEVICE TYPE 'sbt' PARMS 'ENV=(BACKUPSET_DUPLEX=3)';
```

This will configure the backup channel to use the third level of duplix-
ing, which means that RMAN will compare backup blocks to identify
duplicates and only store unique blocks.

It's worth noting that while Advanced Compression and Deduplication can help to optimize storage utilization and performance, they
do come with some trade-offs. Compression can increase CPU usage and potentially slow down write operations, while deduplication
can increase backup and restore times due to the additional processing required to identify and remove duplicates. Organizations should
carefully evaluate the benefits and drawbacks of these features before
deploying them in production environments.

6.15   What are the key performance considerations when implementing Oracle Real Application Clusters (RAC) for high availability and load balancing?

Oracle Real Application Clusters (RAC) is a technology that allows multiple instances of Oracle Database to access a single database simultaneously, providing high availability and load balancing. When implementing RAC, some key considerations for performance include:

1. Network Configuration: In a RAC environment, nodes communicate with each other using a high-speed interconnect. The network configuration must be optimized to ensure that the interconnect has sufficient bandwidth and low latency to avoid bottlenecks.

2. Storage Configuration: Storage plays a critical role in RAC performance. It is important to ensure that the storage subsystem can handle the I/O requirements of the database workload. Careful consideration should be given to the number and speed of disks, RAID level, and disk layout. Also, the database files should be distributed across all storage devices in order to balance the I/O workload among nodes.

3. Instance Configuration: When configuring RAC instances, it is important to ensure that resources are properly allocated to each instance. Each instance should have sufficient memory and CPU resources to handle the workload assigned to it. It is also important to configure the database initialization parameters appropriately to achieve optimal performance.

4. Load Balancing: RAC provides load balancing across multiple nodes, but it is important to ensure that the workload is distributed evenly across nodes. If one node is overloaded, it can affect the performance of the entire cluster.

5. Backup and Recovery: In a RAC environment, backup and recovery operations must be carefully planned to ensure that all nodes and database files are properly backed up and restored.

6. Monitoring and Tuning: Regular monitoring and tuning of the RAC environment is essential to ensure optimal performance. Performance metrics such as CPU usage, memory usage, I/O throughput, and network latency should be monitored regularly to identify and address potential issues.

Overall, proper planning and configuration are essential for optimal performance in a RAC environment. By addressing these key considerations, database administrators can ensure that RAC provides the necessary high availability and load balancing capabilities while also achieving optimal performance.

6.16 Can you explain how to use Oracle's Flashback technologies, such as Flashback Query, Flashback Table, and Flashback Database, in advanced data recovery scenarios?

Oracle's Flashback technologies provide powerful tools for data recovery in advanced scenarios, allowing you to recover lost data even after it has been deleted or modified. In this answer, I'll describe the three main Flashback technologies – Flashback Query, Flashback Table, and Flashback Database – and explain how they can be used to recover data.

Flashback Query: Flashback Query allows you to view data as it existed at an earlier point in time, using the AS OF TIMESTAMP or AS OF SCN clause in a SQL query. This can be useful for recovering data that has been accidentally deleted or modified, as it allows you to see the values of data at the specific point in time before it was lost. For example, let's say that an employee table is accidentally modified at 2:00pm, and you want to recover the data as it existed at 1:00pm. Using Flashback Query, you can run the following SQL query:

```
SELECT *
FROM employees
AS OF TIMESTAMP TO_TIMESTAMP('2021-11-01 13:00:00', 'YYYY-MM-DD HH24:MI:SS');
```

This will show you the values of the employee table as they existed at 1:00pm, allowing you to recover the lost data.

Flashback Table: Flashback Table allows you to revert a table to a previous state, using the FLASHBACK TABLE or the DBMS_FLASHBACK package. This can be useful if you want to recover data from a specific point in time, or if you want to undo a mass update or delete operation. For example, let's say that a mass delete operation was run on the employee table, and you want to recover the deleted data. Using Flashback Table, you can run the following SQL command:

```
FLASHBACK TABLE employees TO BEFORE DROP;
```

This will revert the employee table to its state prior to the drop operation, allowing you to recover the deleted data.

Flashback Database: Flashback Database allows you to recover an entire database to a previous point in time, using the RMAN utility. This can be useful if there has been a catastrophic failure of your database, or if you want to recover from a point in time that is not covered by your regular backup strategy. For example, let's say that there is a major issue with your database at 2:00pm, and you want to recover the database to its state at 1:00pm. Using Flashback Database, you can run the following RMAN command:

```
FLASHBACK DATABASE TO TIMESTAMP TO_TIMESTAMP('2021-11-01 13:00:00', 'YYYY-MM-
    DD HH24:MI:SS');
```

This will recover the entire database to its state as it existed at 1:00pm, allowing you to recover any data that was lost due to the issue at 2:00pm.

Overall, Oracle's Flashback technologies provide powerful tools for data recovery in advanced scenarios, allowing you to recover data at the level of a single SQL query or an entire database. By understanding the capabilities of these technologies, you can ensure that your data is protected against accidental or malicious data loss.

6.17   How do you design and manage efficient, scalable, and fault-tolerant Oracle Data Guard configurations for mission-critical environments?

Oracle Data Guard is a powerful technology that enables organizations to meet a wide range of IT challenges such as managing downtime, reducing risk, and improving disaster recovery. In a mission-critical environment, Data Guard can be instrumental in ensuring the high availability of critical Oracle databases. Below I will explain how to design and manage an efficient, scalable, and fault-tolerant Oracle Data Guard configuration for such environments.

Designing an efficient Data Guard configuration

To design an efficient Data Guard configuration, consider the following:

1. **Network Bandwidth**: The network bandwidth between the primary and standby databases is crucial for efficient Data Guard replication. A fast and reliable network connection is recommended for optimum performance.

2. **File System**: Consider using a balanced file system to prevent bottlenecks. Using a file system that evenly distributes the I/O is optimal.

3. **Disk Space**: Sufficient disk space must be available on the standby host. The standby database should have enough disk space to accommodate any data growth.

4. **Redo transport methods**: Use high-performance options for the redo transport mode, maximum protection, and maximum availability are the recommended options for mission-critical environments. Maximum availability provides zero downtime failover, while maximum protection ensures that no data loss occurs.

5. **Standby configuration**: Consider using a physical standby database configuration for maximum replication efficiency. A physical standby database provides faster switchover and failover, and it is

better suited for high transaction volume.

Managing a scalable and fault-tolerant Data Guard configuration

To manage a scalable and fault-tolerant Data Guard configuration, consider the following:

1. **Performance Monitoring**: Monitor the performance of the primary and standby databases to ensure optimal performance. The primary database should be monitored for resource contention, CPU usage, and disk I/O. The standby database should be monitored for replication lag and any issues with the redo transport.

2. **Disaster Recovery Testing**: Regular testing of the disaster recovery configuration is essential. It is imperative to test the ability to failover to the standby database and come back up immediately.

3. **Regular Patching**: Regular patching of the primary and standby databases is necessary to fix any bugs and security issues. The patches should be applied during a low traffic period to avoid disruptions.

4. **Regular backups**: Regular backups of the primary and standby databases provide an added level of protection. In mission-critical environments, consider performing backups at more frequent intervals.

5. **Automated Monitoring**: Set up automated monitoring of the Data Guard configuration. It will provide notification of replication errors, lag, and other critical issues.

In conclusion, designing and managing an efficient, scalable, and fault-tolerant Oracle Data Guard configuration for mission-critical environments requires careful consideration of various aspects such as network bandwidth, file system, disk space, and redo transport modes. Sufficient performance monitoring, disaster recovery testing, regular patching, regular backups, and automated monitoring are crucial for managing such configurations.

6.18 Can you discuss advanced PL/SQL optimization techniques, such as result caching, pipelined functions, and native compilation, and their impact on performance?

In this answer, we will cover the following topics:

1. Result caching: Caching query results instead of executing them every time can greatly improve performance.

2. Pipelined functions: Processing data in a pipeline rather than all at once can reduce memory requirements and increase performance.

3. Native compilation: Compiling PL/SQL code to machine code can speed up execution times.

Let's dive into each of these topics in more detail.

Result caching

Oracle Database can cache the results of queries that are executed frequently using the Result Cache feature. When a query is executed, its result set can be cached in the SGA (System Global Area) so that the next time the same query is executed, the result can be retrieved from the cache instead of executing the query again.

This can greatly improve performance for queries that are executed frequently and are resource-intensive. By caching the results, we can avoid executing the query every time it is requested, which can save CPU and I/O resources.

To enable Result Cache for a query, we can use the 'RESULT_CACHE' hint. For example:

```
SELECT /*+ RESULT_CACHE */ col1, col2 FROM my_table;
```

We can also configure the Result Cache at the system-level using the 'result_cache_max_size' parameter. This parameter specifies the maximum amount of memory that can be used for caching query results.

Pipelined functions

Pipelined functions are PL/SQL functions that return a collection of
rows instead of a single value. The rows are processed in a pipeline
fashion, meaning they are sent to the caller as soon as they are pro-
duced, rather than waiting for the entire collection to be generated.

This approach can reduce memory requirements and improve performance, especially for large datasets. By processing the data in a
pipeline fashion, we can avoid loading the entire dataset into memory
at once, which can be resource-intensive.

Here's an example of a pipelined function:

```
CREATE OR REPLACE FUNCTION get_employees RETURN emp_tab PIPELINED IS
   emp_rec emp%ROWTYPE;
BEGIN
   FOR emp_rec IN (SELECT * FROM emp) LOOP
     PIPE ROW(emp_rec);
   END LOOP;
   RETURN;
END;
```

In this example, the function returns a collection of 'employee' records
from the 'emp' table. The 'PIPELINED' keyword specifies that the
function is pipelined.

Native compilation

Native compilation is a feature that allows PL/SQL code to be com-
piled into machine code, rather than interpreted by the Oracle Database.
This can speed up execution times by orders of magnitude, especially
for code that is executed frequently or is resource-intensive.

To use native compilation, we need to have the Oracle Database Advanced Security Option installed and enabled. We also need to have
a C compiler installed on the database server.

To compile a PL/SQL program natively, we can use the 'CREATE OR
REPLACE [FUNCTION|PROCEDURE] ... COMPILE PLSQL_CCFLAGS
= '-g -O3 -march=native'' statement. Here's an example:

```
CREATE OR REPLACE FUNCTION my_function(n IN NUMBER) RETURN NUMBER
   COMPILE PLSQL_CCFLAGS = '-g -O3 -march=native' AS
BEGIN
   -- Code here
END;
```

In this example, we're compiling the 'my_function' PL/SQL function natively using the '-g -O3 -march=native' compiler flags.

Conclusion

In conclusion, there are several advanced PL/SQL optimization techniques that we can use to improve performance. Result caching allows us to cache frequently-executed query results in memory, Pipelined functions allow us to process data in a pipeline fashion, improving memory usage, and Native compilation allows us to compile PL/SQL code to machine code, speeding up execution times.

6.19   What are the key considerations when implementing Oracle's Sharding technology for global, large-scale data distribution and management?

Oracle Sharding is a feature introduced in Oracle Database 12c Release 2 (12.2) that allows distributing data across a group of independent databases (shards) while maintaining a single logical database. Sharding enables horizontal scaling and provides high availability and fault tolerance for large-scale applications.

When implementing Oracle Sharding for global, large-scale data distribution and management, there are several key considerations to keep in mind. These considerations include:

1. Data distribution strategy: To distribute data across shards, a data distribution strategy should be defined that takes into account the data access patterns of the application. Oracle provides several built-in data distribution methods such as key-based, range-based, and hash-based. The choice of data distribution strategy can impact performance, maintenance, and scalability of the sharded environment.

2. Shard topology: In a sharded environment, shard topology determines how the individual shards are connected to form a distributed database. Oracle supports several shard topologies such as simple,

composite, and hierarchical. It is important to choose a shard topology that provides high availability, fault tolerance, and scalability.

3. Shard management: Managing shards in a global environment can be complex. Automation and tools should be used wherever possible to minimize human error and reduce operational costs. Oracle provides several tools such as the sharding advisor and the sharding monitor that can help in managing and monitoring sharded environments.

4. Application design: The application design must be modified to work with sharded databases. The application should be aware of the sharding strategy and topology and should be designed to route queries and transactions to the appropriate shards. Oracle provides several APIs and drivers that can help in designing sharded applications.

5. Security: Data security and compliance should be one of the top considerations when implementing sharded databases. Encryption should be used to protect data in transit and at rest. Access controls should be reviewed to ensure that sensitive data is only accessible by authorized users.

6. Disaster recovery and backup: Backup and recovery strategies must be in place to protect against data loss and minimize downtime. Disaster recovery plans must be put in place to ensure business continuity in case of a disaster. Oracle provides several tools such as RMAN and Data Guard that can be used to implement backup and recovery and disaster recovery strategies.

In summary, when implementing Oracle Sharding for global, large-scale data distribution and management, it is important to carefully consider data distribution strategy, shard topology, shard management, application design, security, and disaster recovery and backup. This will ensure high availability, fault tolerance, and scalability of the sharded environment while maintaining data security and compliance.

6.20 How do you use Oracle's Resource Manager and Database Consolidation features to optimize resource utilization, manage workloads, and ensure high performance in a multi-tenant environment?

In a multi-tenant environment, it's essential to optimize resource utilization, manage workloads, and ensure high performance to deliver high-quality services to end-users. Oracle's Resource Manager and Database Consolidation features provide effective means to achieve these goals.

Resource Manager allows you to manage resources in a database instance based on resource groups, resource plans, and directives. Resource groups represent collections of users, application services, or packages that have similar resource requirements or priorities. Resource plans define the allocation of system resources and service levels for each resource group. Directives specify the actions to be taken if a plan's resource allocation is exceeded. A directive can block or kill a session, or it can switch the session to a lower-priority plan.

Database Consolidation is the process of combining multiple databases into a single database instance, which allows for more efficient management of database resources. With consolidation, multiple databases can run on the same hardware, reducing hardware and maintenance costs while improving resource utilization.

Here are some examples of how Resource Manager and Database Consolidation can be used together to optimize resource utilization, manage workloads, and ensure high performance in a multi-tenant environment:

1. Resource allocation: Depending on the resource requirements of each tenant, you can allocate different resource groups to different tenants. For example, resource group A can have higher CPU and I/O allocation than resource group B. Likewise, resource plans can have different resource allocation depending on the tenant's need. For example, resource plan X can have higher I/O allocation than

resource plan Y.

2. Prioritization: You can prioritize resource groups based on the importance of their workload. For example, resource group A can have higher priority than resource group B. Oracle Resource Manager ensures that higher priority resource groups get more CPU and I/O compared to lower priority ones.

3. Limiting resource usage: You can set limits on the amount of CPU, I/O, or other resources to be used by each tenant. Using Resource Manager, you can enforce these limits and prevent tenants from consuming more than their fair share of resources.

4. Consolidating databases: If you have multiple databases, you can consolidate them into a single database instance. This allows for better management of resources, eliminating the overhead of maintaining multiple databases separately. This can lead to a significant reduction in hardware cost and maintenance.

5. Resource usage tracking: With Resource Manager, you can track resource usage by tenants and identify resource-hungry tenants. Based on the identified tenants and resource usage trends, you can allocate more resources or change resource plans.

In summary, Oracle's Resource Manager and Database Consolidation features are powerful tools that can help you optimize resource utilization, manage workloads, and ensure high performance in a multi-tenant environment. By allocating resources based on tenant needs, enforcing limits on resource usage, and tracking resource usage, you can deliver high-quality services to end-users. Additionally, by consolidating databases, you can reduce hardware and maintenance costs while improving resource utilization.

"Oracle Database: Interview Questions and Answers" is a comprehensive guide designed to help professionals at all levels of expertise navigate the complex world of Oracle databases. This book offers a structured approach to understanding the essential concepts, techniques, and best practices required to work effectively with Oracle databases. With a focus on real-world scenarios and practical examples, the author prepares readers to face interviews and job-related tasks with confidence, while also providing a valuable resource for day-to-day problem-solving and decision-making.

Spanning five sections, from Basic to Guru, the book presents a carefully curated selection of over 100 interview questions, each accompanied by detailed answers and explanations. Readers will be introduced to the fundamentals of Oracle database architecture, SQL, and PL/SQL, before delving into more advanced topics such as performance tuning, high availability, security, and cloud migration. By offering a thorough understanding of Oracle databases, this book empowers IT professionals to excel in their roles, make informed decisions, and stay up-to-date with the ever-evolving Oracle technology landscape.

"Advanced Topics in Database" book series is a comprehensive collection of books that delves deep into the world of databases and SQL. This series is designed to cater to database professionals, enthusiasts, and students who aspire to broaden their knowledge and develop expertise in various database management systems.

ISBN 9798395411945

90000

9 798395 411945